Learning to Love Me

Ordinary Women

with

Extraordinary Stories

© 2015 by Toneal M. Jackson. All rights reserved.

No portion of this book may be reproduced mechanically, electronically, or by any other means, including photocopying, without written permission of the publisher.

It is illegal to copy this book, post it to a website, or distribute it by any other means without permission from the publisher.

ISBN: 978-0-9906361-7-5

Library of Congress Control Number: 2015901871

7601 S. Cicero
Chicago, IL 60652
www.weareaps.com

Table of Contents

Foreword 5

Introduction 7

Amani Jackson 9

I Love Me, I Love Me Not 11

Carolyn Gray 17

Being Good to Me 19

Chelsea Duggan 23

Maintaining Integrity 25

Debra Gaynor 29

Loving Myself 31

Dominique Wilkins 35

Learning to Love Myself 37

E. J. Brock 43

The Reflection 45

Freda Emmons 51

Trudging through the Muck 53

Haleh Rabizadeh Resnick 59

How I Came to Believe in Myself 61

Joyce M. Ross 65

The Power of Hope 67

Joyce Stewart 73

Free to Love Me…………………………………………75

Karen C. Brown……………………………………......79

After Breast Cancer……………………………………81

Kelli Bolton……………………………………………. 87

Know Your Worth……………………………………..89

LaDonna Marie…………………………………………93

Fighting to be Me……………………………………… 95

Michelle Poitier……………………………………......99

To Bring Hope Where There is None……………….101

Norlita Brown……………………………………………105

Lady in the Mirror…………………………………….. 107

Renee Bolton………………………………………….. 113

Never Give Up………………………………………….115

Serena Wadhwa……………………………………….121

Giving Me a Chance……………………………………. 123

Shelia Bell……………………………………………….127

I Remember the Time…………………………………129

Tavetta Patterson………………………………………135

Finding the Me to Love………………………………..137

Toneal M. Jackson………………………………………143

The Most Valuable Lesson Learned………………..145

Conclusion……………………………………………….151

Foreword – Written by: National Bestselling Author Sheila E. Bell

There are so many women who are going through tough times because of how they look at themselves when they look in the mirror. Some may feel unloved and unlovable. As women, we tend to judge ourselves harshly. We can easily point out all of our flaws, whether it's our size, skin color, height, financial circumstances - the list is endless. It seems easier for us to see our imperfections rather than see the greatness that lies within each one of us. Now, I'm not saying we should walk around like we're so high and mighty. What I am saying is that we should love the person who God made us to be. No one is perfect. We all fall short.

Allow the words you speak to be words of encouragement, words of promotion, words of love toward yourself and others. Each morning when God opens your eyes, tell yourself what an amazing human being you are. Speak those words! Take the time to look in the mirror and instead of chastising yourself, tell yourself how beautiful you are. Remind yourself, "God doesn't make junk"!

Whoever happens to be reading this, let me just tell you: There is no one quite like you. No one can do the things you do. No one can be the person you are. You are one of a kind. There may be others who have similar talents and gifts, but each person has their own unique abilities. God loves you. He really does.

Introduction – Written by: International Award-Winning Author Toneal M. Jackson, MBA

I wanted to write this book to serve as a point of inspiration and empowerment for all women. To demonstrate that regardless of age, race, ethnicity, economic or political status, we virtually experience the same issues. And although we may encounter a variety of issues throughout the course of our lives, we are equipped to handle them. No two, problems or people, may look the same, but we are capable of identifying with one another. Greater than that, we can use each other's experiences to assist us in overcoming our own situations.

Many times, it's easy to look at someone else and feel as though they have it all, not knowing the struggle associated with maintaining that lifestyle. My purpose is to show you that, no matter what hand you were dealt, you have the power to transform your tragedies into triumphs. Being of the belief that we are better together, I took the liberty of reaching out to some of my friends who share my perspective, and also wanted to provide encouragement.

Combined, the contributors reside in 12 different states; one is from a totally different country. We differ in age, race, professional background, and social status. However, despite the actual hardship, the thread that binds us is that, like you, we are all ordinary women, with extraordinary stories.

Amani Jackson – VA
www.amanijackson.com

Since she was young Amani Jackson wanted to write. Amani is the author of three books, including the recently released, *Conversations That Make A Difference: Shift Your Beliefs To Get What You Want*. She is also the founder of Queendom Magazine.

Aside from writing, she speaks for events or organizations on topics of concern such as teen development, education and women. Her blog, located on her website, shares tips for writers, motivation for entrepreneurs and encouragement for all in between. Out of an interest to see adults expand their perception and cultural exposure, she began Read with Amani, a reading group that meets every other Thursday on her website to discuss selected books. A current resident of Northern Virginia, Amani is single, has no children and enjoys travel.

I Love Me, I Love Me Not
Amani Jackson

I can only recall the darkness. My eyes were open, yes. But the place I found myself in was without light, hopeless. Where was I and how had I gotten here? More importantly, where was the exit?! At 28, bad relationships, coupled with unwise decisions, had finally taken their toll on my mind, body and spirit. I needed salvation, quickly.

The root cause of the problem was that I wanted to be something different from what I was for so much of my life. If I were thinner, lighter, taller, smarter… anything but me…I would be acceptable. My inability to accept myself was so destructive. I felt less than.

Although it was of little comfort, I was a smart girl. Everyone always said it. I was my parents' pride when it came to academics. A child of many passions, they constantly tried to get me to focus on a limited few. It never happened. My entire pre-college life was spent studying, participating in extracurricular activities and doing community service. Yet, this wasn't enough. There was something missing. It didn't provide me what I sought. Guys didn't care about a girl's intellect. I imagined they viewed it as either too challenging or a bore.

In my younger years, my obsession with acceptance was internal. I wanted to like me. Only after entering college did the need for male validation of my worth rear its ugly head. I had the pleasure of experiencing a very fulfilling and supportive relationship once, my high school sweetheart. It was all rainbows and unicorns until it wasn't. Unfortunately, we were very young and immature. Neither of us were well versed enough to handle the conflicts and strains we started dealing with and things fell apart. I chased the ghost of that relationship well into my twenties, praying that someday I would find someone else who loved me with that purity and depth.

My happiness became dependent upon whether or not I was seeing someone. If I was single, I was miserable and empty. My needs banging against each other inside of me, making too much noise, keeping me fully aware of them at all times. If I was with a guy who showed potential, I was elated. I admit it was truly pathetic. However, I could not find solace without companionship. I craved a partner to share the highlights and drama of my day with when it was time to unwind.

This search led me into my marriage, which lasted less than two years. At 22, I was divorced and still miserably in love with my high school sweetheart. My days, and nights, were occupied with the search for an equivalent of what we shared. Sadly, all I acquired was empty relationship after empty relationship. How was it that there were so many dang frogs to kiss!? In truth, like was attracting like. These men had their own demons they warred with and here I was bringing mine into the mix. I didn't love myself and the only men I could be with didn't seem to love themselves either. Perhaps this was a defense mechanism that manifested. Maybe if I had been with a guy who was all the way together, he would call me out on my issues and challenge me to mature and live up to my potential.

Even when I dated a man I knew was not for me, I pined for him. How incredibly desperate and foolish! There was no genuine desire for him or a future with him but I had less of a desire for rejection. I rejected me. Having another person do it was confirmation of my worthlessness. The more degrading a situation I allowed myself to be in the more feverishly I worked at salvaging it. To be dismissed under those circumstances would be unbearable. As things began to unravel, because they always did, I would cling to any clues that suggested there was potential for reconciliation. Any verbal or physical signs were highlighted and honed in on. I would grovel or concede just to appease. It was never worth it.

I put men before my professional and academic responsibilities as well. Going in to work late or missing class, if things were awry in my relationship I had to address before I could move on to anything else or focusing was impossible. Things would easily spiral out of control for me and when the dust cleared, the guys always left unscathed while I put out fires and bandaged the shattered pieces of me.

During those years I fought to love myself. Sure, there were days when my hair was cute or my outfit made me feel glorious, but the feeling was unstable. It didn't stick. The occasional two or three day spurt would occur when I felt good about myself. I loved me. Then it was back to I love me not. I used to wonder if my opinions of myself were shaped by the standards of beauty set in music videos and T.V. shows. However I knew that was naïve. Women had insecurities way before cable.

I compromised and settled when it came to others loving me. In this, I got damaged in ways I felt were beyond repair. I was scared to say no, scared to set boundaries or standards and enforce them. The last thing I wanted was to make it hard for a person to be with me especially since so many other women made it so easy.

My pursuit of love continued. Who would love me? When would this love find me? I needed to fill a void inside of myself and my heart told me that the love of a man was the answer. It was my hope and prayer that each first date would be the last frog I kissed, and upon opening my eyes, my prince would be before me. To my dismay, time after time, the frog remained the frog. It seemed the men I came in contact with were fluent in the language of deceit and skilled in the art of infidelity. I was over it. I was over me.

I consider jaded an amicable term to define how this transformed me. By my mid-twenties I was so skeptical of people's intentions and character that I formed a nasty habit of sabotaging relationships, including ones that could have been valuable. But hindsight is 20/20 and second chances are not guaranteed.

It got so bad for me that I started driving people away. My wall was high, my moat was deep and I was on patrol 25/8. If I heard of or saw another female in my boyfriend's life, immediately I concocted some elaborate, passionate love affair or conversation between the two. This fabrication somehow became reality for me and the barrage of interrogation commenced. I had to be a default, a stand in for his true desire because, for some reason, she was currently unobtainable for him. In my mind, I wasn't good enough to be anyone's one and only, let alone their first choice.

Despite how many people admired something about me, when I looked in the mirror I failed to find beauty. I was chubby and short with average features. Average. Not odd enough to spark interest, not lovely enough to gain admiration. Was there a mistake here? Absolutely. I could only see my flaws. Who doesn't have them? We forget what may be a flaw to one is an asset to another. We see it all the time. A woman might hate her legs but her man adores them. Still, I didn't like myself at all and it showed, making it very challenging for someone else to break past that to like me.

What I came to the full comprehension of later in life, after it bit me in the rear a few times, is that we are our own worst enemy. My insecurities were blaringly apparent. Looking back over some of my relationships, perhaps they were genuinely interested, until the jealousy showed up, the anxieties, and the emotional monsoons. How beautiful she is to look upon until the ugliness is unleashed. What is on the inside always comes out and it can be a game changer.

Then I realized a pattern. What attracted most people to me was my creativity, my way of thinking, my aura. Unfortunately, over the course of the relationship, I neglected 'me' to nurture in an attempt to preserve 'us'. I found myself trying to adopt the persona and behaviors of whoever and whatever I thought pleased them the most. All the qualities that pulled them to me were fading, a memory, and their interest followed suit. While all along I was perfectly desirable before I started fixing what wasn't broken.

The moment I grasped this I decided to live according to it. So what, I have more curves than some women. I'm amazing. I no longer care that I'm short. A shirt I once read said that God only let's things grow until they are perfect. Guess I was done early. And yes, I fight to control my jealousy and dictator-like behavior, but at least there is no denial and I'm making strides daily…okay maybe monthly…let's just say it's happening.

Carolyn Gray – Spring, TX
www.zirconsulting.com

Carolyn Gray is a Human Resources Consultant with expertise in building personal and professional relationships. She is the owner of Zircon Consulting, a boutique consulting/training firm in Spring, Texas that specializes in relationship coaching, HR (employee/labor relations) personal development, relationship building, business etiquette and customized training based on organizational needs.

She is a certified professional coach and Personality Assessment Trainer, speaker, etiquette consultant and internationally recognized author.

Carolyn enjoys golfing, reading and traveling. She is married and has one son, a daughter and son-in-love and two grandsons.

Being Good to Me
Carolyn Gray

When I think about treating me good, I am reminded of years of me making sure that others in my life had what they wanted and needed without giving much thought to what I wanted or needed. What I noticed was I was doing unto to others and not much for me.

I felt I loved me; however, I was more often than not putting others first. Then, one day, while traveling from the east coast to the west coast, hearing the familiar words of the flight attendant, "put your mask on first", resonated with me. That was not my first time hearing those words; however it was the first time I thought of them having anything to do with me and how I relate to others.

It was long flight so I had time to think about how I could make "putting my mask on first" work in my life. Going from thoughts like, "that's selfish" or "am I totally abandoning the Golden Rule" to "how could I be more beneficial to others if I took care of myself first".

I prayed for guidance because I wanted to continue to serve others in love and did not want to feel that I was being selfish. I analyzed myself and felt I was honest, compassionate, friendly, fair, loving, kind and giving and that is what I wanted to continue to be. I told myself that making this change would help me better serve others.

After much thought while on that flight, I concluded that I had to take control of doing unto me as I do unto others, in other words, I had to learn to put my mask on first. In doing that, I had to learn to say "no" sometime and I had to stop trying to be everything to everyone. Not turn my back on others, just put my mask on first.

What could I do to demonstrate to myself that I was putting my mask on first? Well, I decided to be aware of and take steps to have better health. I started by having a complete physical exam and committing to do so annually. I scheduled a time to exercise and stuck to that schedule as often as possible (I even traveled with my handheld bar bells so I could exercise in my hotel room)! I did not let the voice in my head tell me that I was tired and I could exercise tomorrow. If someone asked me to do something for them, I would not let that little voice keep me from helping them, and so I had to do the same for myself.

Eating better came right along with exercising. This was actually harder than staying on an exercise schedule because of my family's busy schedule. My fix, always have something with me to snack on until I could get a nutritious meal. Did that always work? Absolutely not …I occasionally succumbed to my not so nutritious favorite: fried chicken! I saw this as being A-Okay because it was not something I did on a regular basis.

As a self-proclaimed "night owl," I had to force – FORCE--FORCE—myself to rest. Rest like get at least six hours of sleep each night (six was my magic number!). Most nights I managed to get six hours of sleep and trust me, I could tell the difference the next day if I only got four or five hours of sleep.

Reading has always been a relaxing and enjoyable

pastime for me but I had actually put that aside until I started to put my mask on first. I made a commitment to read at least one book a month for inspiration, pleasure, motivation or self-help. This is a commitment I do not let anything stop me from doing. I always have something in my purse, or on my smart phone to read. I can read in short spurts (waiting to see my physician, at the post office or traveling) and I enjoy reading most genres. I love children's books. I have recently been introduced to the Llama Llama books because they are my two year old grandson's good reads.

Doing unto me has allowed me to write several books, complete a 365 day expression of gratitude where I publically expressed gratitude for 365 days about people, places, books or situations that have helped me to be the person I am today. Expressing gratitude, written and/or spoken has been one of the most rewarding experiences I have had. Being grateful has been good for my overall being.

I do unto others; I just do unto me first in order for others to experience a more enriched and loving person and that person is me.

Chelsea Duggan – Highland Park, IL
www.milestarbabies.com

Chelsea Duggan is an entrepreneur, parent and advocate for early childhood development through creative education. She is the Founder and Director of Milestar Babies, an educational program whose curriculum focuses on encouraging children to discover, synthesize, and create.

She is a graduate of Northwestern University, a member of the Chicago Startup Leadership Program, and the Founding Moms.

Chelsea loves creating learning adventures with her three young boys, practicing roundhouse kicks, and crafting culinary delights using butter, chocolate and sugar.

Maintaining Integrity
Chelsea Duggan

I sat at her feet, half listening to the buzz of the television while riding the roller coaster of sound in my head – some clarinet sonata not yet under my fingers. A soft kick brought me back too, and the pleasant request for a cup of tea and the requisite piece of coffee cake.

Whistling along with the kettle, I licked a crumb from my finger as I sought to balance two plates and one steaming cup.

Having delivered our snack, I sat back down as my Gram clicked off the television. She wanted to unfold a story – one of many – I would come to know over shared afternoons. This one was different though as the precursor of silence predicted.

Having been kicked out of the house, I spent my days working with the mannequins, dressing them for parties that would never happen. After work, I dragged my feet over to Michelle's. She was lovely to let me stay at hers while Sam had his ear to his sister's tall tales. Tangled tales that could make you blush with their indecency and untruth. Thankfully, Michelle helped me clear my mind if only by scooting out the door to go dancing shortly after I'd arrived. Days were repeated without fanfare. So I took a chance. I called Sam.

He told me in simple words to come to the house to collect my things.

The day was filled with anticipation that made the

bottom of my stomach ache like I hadn't eaten for days. Food looked like rocks and my fists were already weighted down from the monotony of work and the strength with which it took to keep from shaking. I hadn't even made it through lunch. The day continued with the only reprieve being sent on an errand to fetch some new samples from a tailor across town. Finally, a chance for my first breath of the day.

He told me in simple words to come to the house to collect my things.

The afternoon ticked by as if each second had to declare its place in time. I knew in my heart that I had not disobeyed my vows. The thin stretch of white gold only told the truth even if time had dulled its luster. I wish I could say the same for my sister-in-law. Her tongue was sharp with colloquial Italian that made my head swim as if underwater. I would always swim upstream when it came to her.

The house was dark and quiet. The two steps up to the door did nothing to elevate my strength. No need for a deep breath – just push the bell and the chime will dictate my fate.

"You're here. I suppose you want to collect your things".

"Sam, I didn't cheat…"
"Your things are out back". The door closed resolutely.

He told me in simple words to come to the house to collect my things.

I could smell the tang before my eyes adjusted to the low flames. The phantom shapes of prized possessions lay wilted from the heat. My wedding gown with only a touch of white showcased from what looked like a sleeve. Rectangles maintained their clear shape even though the photos and finishes had long evaporated. The fire had clearly been burning for several hours. Everything I had ever touched, possessed, remembered was destroyed. There was nothing left of my past. I had fallen in the forest. I turned for home, resolutely.

"Things don't matter. What matters is that you maintain your integrity. You work hard, you do right by yourself, and everything will turn out okay". She slurped the last of her tea and the clink of the cup echoed. What could I respond after a story like that. Initially, it made me hate the grandfather I had never met. Those feelings faded and with the setting of the story came a new sunrise.

My Gram was a huge inspiration for me in learning to love myself. Her story taught me that I had to depend on myself first. I make every effort to set myself up for success. I do this by showing up and doing my homework. Choose what you want to do and then educate yourself on what steps you need to take to reach your goal. Hold yourself accountable and don't be afraid to ask for help along the way. I also try to give help where I can every day. It can be as simple as letting someone go ahead of me in traffic, listening to a friend, or connecting others. I learned that if you give first, it will be easier when you need to ask for help. I've learned to love myself through taking care of myself (physically, spiritually, and emotionally) so that I can give to others freely.

Debra Gaynor – Hawesville, KY
www.bookreviewsbydebragaynor.com

Debra Gaynor is a Christian still growing in Christ. She is the former CEO of Readers' Favorite, the fastest growing book review and award contest site on the Internet (www.readersfavorite.com). The company earned the respect of renowned publishers like Random House, Simon & Schuster, and Harper Collins, and received the Best Websites for Authors and Honoring Excellence awards from the Association of Independent Authors.

Currently, she reads and reviews books of various genres. In addition to reviewing books, she enjoys reading, writing, cooking. Debra and her husband have three children and twelve grandchildren. She and her husband live on a farm in a small town in Kentucky.

Loving Myself
Debra Gaynor

Early in life I discovered that I wanted to please people. There is nothing wrong with that as long as you also learn to stand on your principles and not allow others to take advantage of you. I spent the first 55 years of my life attempting to please someone, anyone, and yes everyone. I wanted to please my parents, my teachers, my friends, my husband, my children and God. I was self-defeating in the process of pleasing others. I realize that sounds like a contradiction and perhaps I am a person with contradicting needs. I felt that I was bouncing off of walls in an effort to be perfect. When I couldn't meet that goal I would throw up my hands and tell myself, "I just can't do this anymore"!

I was short in stature. Even when I started first grade at 5 years old I was small. It was 1960 and our area did not have pre-school or Kindergarten and, even if they'd had it my family could never have afforded it. I was the smallest one in my class. I weighed about 31 pounds and was about 32 inches tall. The other kids at school looked at me as if I was a much younger kid. Although I can understand their thinking, at five years of age, it still hurts to feel left out.

I never truly felt I fit in anywhere and I tried too hard. Like most people I wanted to fit in. I hated school! It was a social thing. I was the kid that would drop her pencil, lean over to pick it up and then drop everything else. I was clumsy, uncoordinated and socially inept.

At the beginning of each school year I would be

determined to study hard and make the grades but I was easily self-defeated and soon quit trying. This was a pattern that I developed and it followed me into adulthood.

I felt guilty if I didn't spend "enough" time with my family and friends. It seemed I was always volunteering to take someone to the doctor. It is not that I regret doing that but I was doing it for the wrong reasons. I needed the positive feedback to make me feel good about myself. My sense of self-worth was like a yo-yo going up and down according to the feedback of others.

I never felt pretty. When I looked in the mirror I saw a round face with eyes too small and a nose with a ball on the end. My thighs were too heavy, my waist wasn't small enough and I was too short. The simplest criticism would destroy me.

My relationship with the Lord was affected by my self-doubts. I found myself trying to do things that would please God rather than wait on Him to lead. I found myself singing in the choir, leading committees, and feeling guilty if I missed church on a Sunday morning, Sunday evening and Wednesday night.

For approximately 25 years I taught an adult Sunday school class. I loved it and I was good at it. However, I felt guilty if I missed a daily devotional, bible reading, prayer time or grace. Of course all of these things are important but they are not and should not be "mandatory".

My goal was to please God. How could I do it? I tried to be perfect for him but kept falling short.

I am a decent public speaker and it dawned on me that I could help God out by becoming a Lay speaker. I found myself speaking in many churches in our area. I enjoyed it very much. I was good at lay speaking. However, I still felt that tugging of the Holy Spirit. In my infinite wisdom (not) I thought I could help God out even more if I became a Pastor. It was a total disaster. I was not called to be a pastor; once again I had attempted to "help" God.

However, along my journey of learning to love me I discovered a few tips:

1. It is ok to say no. It is ok to place my needs first and to spend time doing what I want even if that means not helping someone with something.
2. It is ok not to be perfect. I can set goals for myself and work toward them but it is also ok if I stumble and fall.
3. I am not responsible for everyone else's wants and needs.
4. Each day is a new beginning.
5. I am worth the effort.
6. I am responsible for my attitude and happiness.
7. If I can't love and respect me how can I expect anyone else to love and expect me?
8. I must learn to accept who I am fully, both the good and the bad.

9. I must make the effort to change me because I want to change not because someone else wants me to change but because it is part of healthy personal growth.

10. I must be totally honest with myself.

11. I must set aside time for ME.

12. It is ok to ask for help if I need it.

13. I must give thanks for <u>ALL</u> things.

14. I must forgive myself. We all make mistakes and it is time to stop beating myself up.

15. As I grow spiritually I will come to love myself. I will have peace; I will feel connected; I will be kinder, more loving and more compassionate.

16. I must take care of my health.

17. I need to have fun and not take myself too seriously.

18. I must enjoy the beauty around me.

It took 55 years to discover that I did not have to do anything for God. He doesn't need my help. I don't have to do anything to make Him love me because He loves me just as I am with my quirks and self-doubt and all my other flaws. Isn't that amazing!

He created me in his image. He set me free to be me. It is not a sin to love myself, especially if I can simply love the self that was created.

Dominique Wilkins – Elkhart, IN
www.authordwilkinsgoodbooks.com

Dominique Wilkins is a licensed cosmetologist, and an author of short stories in the Urban Christian Fiction genre. She employs her practical experience to transfer years of emotional support from the beauty salon to her books. She writes to encourage readers and provide them with resources to keep them going and give them a desire to do better.

She currently has over 25 published works all tackling some of life's toughest issues (including parenting and infidelity) and giving The Word of God to stand on in the outcomes. Her stories are written with biblical scriptures intermingled for the reader to reference or research for more healing directly from The Bible. Dominique has learned that her life is nonexistent without His grace, mercy and love. Her message of Living Life with a Purpose is geared toward everyone!

Learning to Love Myself
Dominique Wilkins

I was a sheltered nerd, whose only companion necessary for the first 10 years of my life, was a good book. School was a great place to display my leadership capabilities, so all of the way through 8th grade, I was one of the best of the best; most likely to succeed if they ever took a vote.

I graduated with so many awards my mother came with gym shoes on prepared to stand for the entire time as they read my achievements. I earned a $50 savings bond and a letter from Bill Clinton- the sitting president at the time; I even gained the acceptance into Whitney Young High School (First Lady, Michelle Obama's alma mater), one of the top schools in Chicago. Though I had everything, I actually had nothing, which I didn't wake up and realize until later.

After 8th grade graduation, I spent most of my teenage and young adult life chasing love or at least twisted versions of what I thought it was. I'm sure it was an obvious signal to others that I had no self-love because of how much time I spent trying to find a man to love me. It did not matter how much my mother, father, brothers or sisters loved me, I thought I needed a man to validate me. Everyone else had a boyfriend to claim them and show them affection, so I felt I needed that too.

I was so smart; I knew that if I used my body, I would cut out a lot of time playing games and guys would love me because I wasn't stingy with it. Then I'd show them that I was faithful; I had a plan and I was working it. Sadly, I was teaching a lesson to the onlookers that book smarts were not remotely the same as street smarts. I did a lot of car hopping and gangsta chasing, I was in the streets more than I was out of them, and had started to slowly learn what the saying "if you live by the streets, you die by the streets" meant. There was this incident where my "gangster boyfriend" pulled a gun on me and shoved it in my face, had his way with me and held me hostage until he was good and ready to set me free. After going into my own witness protection program, I began to focus on a less thuggish type of guy.

In my freshman year of college, I was working and putting myself through school. By then, my behavior caused my mother so much pain, she no longer felt that I was a remarkable investment, and decided to save her money to pay for bills and emergencies instead of my college education.

While attempting to redeem myself, I fell for an upper classman on the basketball team. He was mine and I was his, it didn't matter that he never did anything for me nor could he afford to do so. I had enough excuses to cover any question a hater would pose!

He couldn't get a job, because his coach wanted them to focus only on basketball. He didn't wear any real clothes because he was always playing ball. He didn't need a car because our school was located in the middle of the loop, where only a fool would dare to drive. I'd never been a materialistic girl; all I ever needed was a person's love and that was free. So, I had no problem buying him everything he needed: phone, clothes, food, shoes, hotel stays, restaurants, and even a pager. When the cash money ran out, a creditor educated and provided me a pin number in order to obtain cash advances from my credit cards.

Life was good. I had a job down the street from home and a steady boyfriend at school. But one day, I became so sick at work, I left early and even called off extra days. I missed so many, that of course I lost my perfect job. I went to the hospital, and was diagnosed with a disease that I'd never be able to get rid of; the doctor told me I was pregnant - only had 5 months left (either the ultrasound picture or the words made me vomit again).

I dropped out of school, because my morning sickness disabled me for a full two months. I found myself a single mother who still hadn't figured out the purpose of self-love and now, I had a child in tow watching my every move. Having a child forced me to grow up. So, when I met a hard-working, blue collar man who gave both me and my son quality time and attention, I decided I would give him an ultimatum to marry us or leave us alone (after six months).

It was clear that he loved me and my son, but even Ray Charles could see that he wasn't in love enough to be fully committed to marriage at that point. But I saw a window of opportunity, and unless he called my bluff and stopped me, I was going to go through with it. I figured whatever gaps or things we needed to work on could be done after the vow exchange.

I was married for twelve years. We had tons of ups and way more downs than I wanted to admit. My mother used to say that the toughest years in a marriage were the first five because you are learning how to respect each other and how to co-exist. She said after you've gotten tired of fighting and trying to change each other, it gets easier because you've learned the concept of choosing your battles in order to maintain peace and harmony at home. However, in our seventh, eighth and ninth year, I began to grow tired. I was tired of bickering and sacrificing. I noticed that my original idea of doing whatever it took to break his barriers and make him feel like a king (so that he would reciprocate and we live happily ever after), was never going to happen.

Instead of him seeing my sincere love for him, his outside children and his parents, he allowed them to come in between us. Toward the end, I began to realize that more and more often, I felt less than happy and loved. Although my husband was a good man, that was not good enough for *me*, because I had yet to discover what it truly meant to love myself.

As my ears began to open and listen to my inner-self begging to be loved or treated fairly, we grew further and further apart. Eventually, the image that I was so proud to have and worked so hard for, no longer seemed worth having. I needed to be happy on the inside and not just from an outsider looking in. I needed to give my tears a break. So when the next argument came, I packed my bags and my children and left.

Alone with my children and my thoughts, I quickly began to see that in my darkest moment, a light began to shine. It got brighter and brighter. The brighter it became, the stronger it made me. Deep down, I always had a fear of being alone. I always thought I needed a man and his love to validate me, but out on my own with no money and no experience of being independent, I felt a strange sense of empowerment. I had only taken one step, but even then, it didn't seem like it would be the last.

It was in my darkest time, when I realized that every decision that I had made on my own was a recipe for disaster, I called out for Him and asked Him to save me…and He obliged. That day, God saved a wretch like me. Each day, as I listen to His voice, I realize that I may be a sinner and may not do everything correctly, but it is always with the best intentions. He knew my heart, and took me out of that situation to show me what REAL love was like. God knew that I spent my whole life looking for love from a man and here He was all along waiting for me to find Him!

It is wonderful, how I feel. I am no longer pained or hurt if someone doesn't like me. I am who I say I am; I set my standards and people *now* like and respect me because I set the bar. I don't change who I am or what I want to do to chase or please anyone else any longer. I read my Bible and I practice what I learn. I pray for God to continue to fix me and forgive me and now, I live the happiest life ever. I realize that I am who I am because Jesus loves me, and because of His love for me, and I now able to love myself!

E. J. Brock – Gary, IN
www.aspiritmateromance.com

E. J. Brock is the acclaimed author of the 5 star 22 book series, **"A Spirit Mate Love Story & Paranormal Romance"**. The premise of her series is derived of two scriptures: **Gen. 6:1** *"The sons of God saw the daughters of men and found them to be fair and they took them wives of all which they chose,"* and, **Jude 1:6** *"And the Angels kept not their first estate."* In this riveting series, she highlights the threefold nature of mankind: Spirit, Soul and Body.

She makes it easy to visualize everyday struggles with spiritual warfare, while succumbing to the flesh. She gives a visible view of the battle between good and evil; angel and demon. All for the souls of God's 'so' loved humanity.

Her series can be classified as Edgy Christian Fiction, because she writes outside the normal Christian Fiction. She captivates her reader's imagination with her literary machinations of that one true love ordained in the Heavens. She leaves you longing for your own **"Spirit Mate"**.

The Reflection
E. J. Brock

I've never been one to chit chat first thing in the morning. My family understands that, and has never been offended to my 'ump' response to their morning greeting. We all have a routine. Those essential things we do, before we face the world. Mine has always been to start my morning with unbridled intimacy; just me and my lover…caffeine!

While in the throes of coming to life, I meditate and give thanks to God. Not only for keeping me all night, and waking me up, but also for my lover…Coffee!

After that I'd start to perk up, and get ready for the day. I'd shower, brush my teeth, put on my makeup, and get dressed. Then I'd comb my hair, and brush my teeth again. Just before I'd leave the confines of my bedroom, I would pause…

I had passed *that* mirror for over thirty years. In fact I'd stand in front of it, and strike one pose after another. Day after day, year after year, I said 'good morning', and it would respond, in kind.

It was my closest friend, and most trusted confidant. Unlike those family members on the other side of my bedroom door, it never required anything from me. It never frustrated me. It never deceived me!

In a voice that was audible only to me, it spoke to my readiness; or lack thereof. I never had to quote, *'mirror, mirror on the wall'*. It was more than willing to freely offer its advice. Year after year I adhered to its counsel, because I knew I could trust it. Some days, like a movie critic, it gave me two thumbs up and I would smile. Other days it said what I didn't want to hear, but I accepted its advice. A few times it kept me trapped in my bedroom for more than a minute. It compelled me to change my outfit five or six times.

Then the day came when *everything* changed. I had followed my routine to the letter. Caffeine, shower, brush teeth, dress, comb hair, and pause. Like a snowball on a hot summer day, my self-confidence, and enthusiasm, melted.

For the first time in over thirty years, my trusted confidant let me down. At first, I thought maybe I was still asleep. I told myself I had to be dreaming, and if I were it was a nightmare. But it wasn't a dream, or nightmare, and I wasn't asleep! I was so devastated I stumbled backwards, and almost lost my balance. I rapidly blinked, to keep from crying.

The image looking back at me could *not* be real! The once youthful image was no more! The hair that once was so black it looked blue…was *all* gray!

The figure that had always been shaped like an hour glass, or a perfect figure eight, was gone! In its place was the image of a torso that looked to be filled with helium. It was an oblong zero, with extremities! Even they had lost their shapeliness. When in the *world* did that happen?

From the time I was sixteen, my breast had always been a solid, perky, and firm, triple D! I used to boast by saying, *"These two girls are the only suckers I trust"* just before I snuggled my money in their protective crevices. Never once did they sag…until that moment!

The once sleek tarsals, that sported the ankle strapped of 5 inch heels, were replaced by puffy blobs. No doubt from years of bearing the burden of carrying the, helium fill, torso.

The eyes looking back at me had always glimmered with a youthful glow, but not now! Now they were weary, and bogged down; undoubtedly by the trials of life.

My voiceless, and now deceitful, confidant began to taunt me. It began to sing, *'The old gray mare ain't what she used to be'*. Then it said, *"Look closer, woman!"* I did and grabbed my mouth, to keep from screaming.

The hair, the body, the eyes; none of it was my image! Yet it stared back at me. I dissected every aspect of the image. I examined the eyes, nose, mouth, hair, and the body; I still refused to see it as me! It wasn't my face. It was Ms. Jodi's face, or as my siblings and I called her *Madea!*

By no means was my mother an ugly woman. However, I do not remember a day in my lifetime, when she wasn't gray, and overweight. In retrospect, she was overweight for good cause. I am the youngest of ten children she graciously allowed to sublet her womb; I guess that many babies will do that to a body!

By the time I reached my teenage years she was already old, *and* tired. All of a sudden, the image looking back at me was too! How in God's name did that happen? I imploded.

For the next six months I refused to look in the glass. I refused to put on makeup. What for? I knew what it would reveal! Something I didn't want to see, or accept.

My co-workers noticed the difference in me; my friends and family did too! My three oldest sisters laughed at me. They gleefully reminded me of a time when I told them *they* were old. They were 32, 33, and 35 at the time. I was *only* 22 years old, and a brick house! But they reminded me that I was almost *twice* the age they were when I'd called them old.

I decided I was going to dye my hair, and take my youth back. I totally forgot what happened to Madea when she attempted the same thing.

When I was nine, Ms. Jodi dyed her hair. She had no idea she was allergic. Her head swelled so big I was afraid of her. She looked like a monster to my nine year old mind. I would not go near her, and it made her cry. Guess who else was allergic to hair dye?

My head had swollen like the Elephant Man's! The follicles in my scalp were on fire. The dye had touched my neck, ears and shoulders; they blistered to the point that I couldn't stand anything to touch them. Bulbous knots were on my cheeks, temple and even my lips. I couldn't even brush my teeth because the pain was unbearable, which was okay, because I wasn't about to leave the house anyway…except to go to the doctor. And even he snickered!

The thick gray hair that I loathed was now black, but it

was falling out in patches; I was really depressed! Lord knows I prayed for death!

I couldn't cry, because the tears would burn my swollen eyes, so I just moaned. Then I remembered my mother's tears, and cried anyway. Not for myself, but for what she must have felt when I was afraid of her.

It took two weeks for the swelling to go down, and for me to get the feeling back in my face. I was so excited I just had to look in that old deceitful mirror. It was depressing to see my once thick hair was now thin, and patchy…and it was *still* my mother's face!

Again, my deceitful, and voiceless, confidant spoke. This time it reprimanded me. "It's been thirty years, Eva. Did you think time would stand still, just for you?

I wiped my tears, while it kept scolding me…

"What is so wrong with getting older, anyway? Your only alternative is dying young."

I stopped crying because the image in the mirror was right! As long as I live, I'm going to age. Tomorrow, today will become *yesterday* and tomorrow will become *today!* Days become weeks; next week, this week becomes *last week!* Weeks become months; next month this month becomes *last month!* Months become years; this year will eventually be called *last year!* And all the while, time will keep slipping into the future.

I made up my mind that day that I was going to do like my mother. I was going to grow old *gracefully.* From that day to this one, I have never again attempted to change who I am. I also made another decision that day - to live with a heart of thanksgiving and a spirit of praise.

All in all I feel good about the winding road I've traveled! From arrogant vanity, to self-loathing, to learning how to *love* myself! And like Paul I've learned that whatever state I find myself therein to be content.
Philippians 4:11

These days when I look in the mirror I am no longer traumatized, but comforted. It is still my mother's face looking back at me, but now it gives me *greater* joy.

Now when I look in the mirror, I smile, and say, "Good morning, Madea".

Freda Emmons – Troutdale, OR
www.flameofhealing.com

Freda Emmons is an author, and inspirational speaker, who grew up suffering the violence of physical and sexual abuse and the severe emotional trauma that accompanies such pain. Freda sought counseling for 12 years and when she began to grow in her Christian faith, she realized the depth of healing in the words of the Bible. She combined tiny steps of healing with those comforting Scriptures and wrote Flame of Healing, which is a devotional with a journal, for in depth, personal healing.

In 2014, Freda began a non-profit, Healing Love Foundation, to raise funds, gather donations and compile Healing Love Packages, which include a Bible, a copy of Flame of Healing, a throw blanket, and a notepad and pen. These packages will be given to individuals who are seeking healing, but cannot afford the book.

Trudging Through the Muck to a Destiny of Love
Freda Emmons

I am a survivor of childhood physical and sexual abuse. Even before I could say "No" or run away, perhaps around one year old, my innocence was shredded. In all, three different people hurt me sexually; my body was beaten and assaulted almost daily in my youth. How does a child survive such overwhelming trauma to her body and soul? I believe the most powerful influence of my survival has been the gracious love of God. The specific ways God helped me were truly miraculous.

I could not see or feel God's love and grace at the time, because I was living a life of daily physical and emotional pain. The first two survival mechanisms were protective separations from the physical and sexual assaults. By God's powerful grace, when the assault occurred, I emotionally went into a black cloud of safety.

My body and emotions separated; the body experiencing pain, but the emotions were protected in the black cloud. The next was simply an extension of the black cloud. I disassociated, separating into two distinct parts of me, the day child (who attended school, interacted with the family and learned the clarinet and Spanish and attended church) and the night child (who held all the secrets and was completely separate until another assault was added to her storage chest of secrets).

The third way God's grace was with me throughout

the years of pain was His provision of people and places which were safe and comforting. I loved school because it was safe and I soaked in every measure of love and acceptance I could receive. I was quite clingy with my friendships because I was so needy of love and acceptance. At the same time, I had no skills of how to be a friend. Yet, there were two friends, in my youth, who gave me the full amount of friendship and love that I needed.

I spent hours and hours at my dear Ruby's house, even eating with her family. They were safe and loving. It was hard to go home; even without expressing to anyone my reluctance to do so. At Ruby's, I was satisfyingly accepted and loved. When Ruby's family moved to another state, I was truly broken emotionally; I couldn't even express how deep my pain was. It just was.

It was merely a few months later, when Sharon came into my life. She moved to my hometown from another state and we were fast friends right from the first moment, I think because of her deep compassion. Quite beyond my perception, Sharon understood my pain and talked with school teachers, counselors and her mother and prepared a plan, to invite me to live with her to get out of the violence of my home.

When she invited me, I was completely unaware of all the preparation, but received the life-line of living in a safe home. All of this happened in about four months, from the day I met her until our friendship became the beginning of my healing. Sharon's home was clean and safe; her family was loving and supportive of me. I struggled with a non-existent self-esteem and had numerous emotional issues, yet Sharon loved me.

I was starved for love and yet, I felt completely unlovable. Looking back to the child I was, I recognize that throughout my young life, I viewed everything through a filter. Many people have a positive filter of how they see things, and think that all of life is good and bad things just don't happen. Others have the opposite filter and are stuck in thinking that everything is rotten in life and nothing good could ever happen.

My filter was that my body resembled ground-up meat, like the sexual assaults I'd endured were as relentless as a voracious meat grinder. However, as a teenager, I could not even begin to identify my feelings; I was too overwhelmed by life. At that time, I was even afraid to ride a bus or make a phone call. It sounds so strange now, but my brokenness was so complete that it affected all aspects of my life.

God's grace was covering me as a young adult, caring for me as a doe tenderly cares for her fawn. I easily could have fallen into a relationship with a fella that would hurt me more; domestic violence often can be traced back to violence in the perpetrator's and/or the victim's family of origin. God's tender love brought to me, in the simplest setting of a college dance, a man of true compassion, tenderness and love.

We met in February, were engaged in three weeks, and married in December of the same year. In many ways, I was completely devoid of life skills. The first few years of adult life, much less married life, were a combination of intense learning, demanding control, and learning to set aside my own likes and dislikes.

My husband, Rod, was patient, loving and supportive; he taught me what love really is - gentleness and always blessing each other. We weathered many storms of life together, financial problems, health issues, and raising children.

As a young mother, I noticed that I was a bit out of control with how I cared for my children. I used the same discipline I had grown up with, hitting the closest part of the kid that was the closest, for whatever problem was a problem for me. I decided I needed to find a better way; I did not want my children to grow up in the violence that I did.

I initiated counseling, which embarked a 12 year trek through the muck, but ultimately helped me to process the pain that I had stuffed way down and kept stuffing with food and more food. As a child, I had learned that food was very comforting, when my world was anything but comfortable. Counseling helped me to begin to address the underlying emotions of my overeating.

I also learned other ways of disciplining my children, without my anger being a part of it. I was able to address the issue without anger and resorting to a physical assault of my child. I had to learn to think about life, family and all of the parenting issues differently.

In the process, I saw with stark clarity how violence had so infiltrated my life that if I was not very careful, I would repeat the same horror upon my children. It was good that I was in counseling, because when I acknowledged this fact, it brought about a new level of self-loathing. Counseling had extremely beneficial aspects, but also brought to my awareness the deep areas of shame and self-deprecation.

A further acknowledgement of reality was rising to the surface of my consciousness; not only had I been a victim of sexual and physical assaults, but I had become a part of the violence. I had beat my younger brothers and in some sick, twisted quirk, I had repeated with my younger brother the sexual act that was done to me.

I had no understanding at the time of how wrong this was, or how damaging it was to my brother. That miserable self-loathing was scraping the bottom of the deep scum of my youth. The only positive aspect is that acknowledgement of the problem is an important step in beginning the healing process.

I went through a season of intense depression. I had completed counseling, but my own participation in the physical and sexual violence was devastating. I began to realize that a lumbering dark cloud hovered over me at the very least, 25 days every month. Every once in a while, I felt the oppression lift, but then it would descend upon me and I was immobilized in self-revulsion. I stayed in it, languishing in a combination of self-pity and abhorrence of my actions. After a long while, I finally decided I didn't want to live that way. I was just beginning a more in-depth walk with my faith in Jesus Christ and had begun to read the Bible daily. I realized it was jammed with love and healing; hope ignited in my soul.

When I processed forgiving myself, I was able to

receive the grace and love Christ has for me. I could begin to love myself. Loving myself was such a new feeling, I needed to practice it. I had spent so many years detesting myself that it would actually be easier to continue in its path of degradation. In order for me to heal completely, I needed to trust that Christ forgave all that was evil in me and loves me and I needed to do the same. After some time, I began to see a turn-around, from living under the oppressive cloud of depression to choosing daily to live a more joyful life.

Haleh Rabizadeh Resnick – Cherry Hill, NJ
www.littlepatientbigdoctor.com

Haleh Rabizadeh Resnick, Esq. is a mom and author of <u>Little Patient Big Doctor</u>. Educated as an attorney, she has also worked as an advisor and teacher to children of all ages.

Like every other woman she knows, she thinks about that home and work life balance and hasn't quite figured out if it's fully possible. While writing her book, she looked up from her computer to see her children running on the roof with a bucket of water, while the sitter waved to them and watched.

Today, she speaks with groups across the country about parenting and health advocacy.

How I Came to Believe in Myself
Haleh Rabizadeh Resnick

I could tell you about the tens of times, I was right and the doctor was wrong. Give it up for mother's intuition.

I could tell you about the time I counted to three and my kids actually jumped to action. Yes THE time. Okay, maybe there've been two or three other times - but that's it.

I could tell you about the time I increased volunteerism ten-fold in my children's school or the time I learned English, graduated law school or wrote my book. Or my favorite, the time I laughed when I saw my kids running up and down the roof with buckets of water - having a water fight. Yes, that actually made me believe in myself just a bit more.

But I won't tell you about any of these times because to be completely honest, they all made me believe in myself but the effects were always temporary. So, that just doesn't count.

No matter what I do, inevitably self-doubt comes right back. Anyone could've done what I did. I was just lucky. Other people have done more than me. I could've done it even better. Okay fine - I did a great job but that was then . . . how about now?

This self-doubt is a killer. And no matter what I do, it always has a way of creeping back. Believing that God has a purpose for us - helpful but I end up doubting anyway. Prayer - helpful but I'm not a holy person. Live in the moment – works - until I step out of it. Exercise – helpful - but so hard to stick to.

Surrounding myself with happy, positive amazing people - helpful until I end up doubtful again. Keeping busy, very helpful - until I crash.

So, how have I come to believe in myself? Here's my secret and I hope it works for you. I've come to accept that I simply don't always believe in myself.

The truth is that we are all imperfect beings. Our goal in life is to perfect ourselves. Don't get me wrong, God created a perfect being, but in our perfection lies imperfection. That's what makes life worth living - okay and makes it absolutely hair ripping too.

Here's the bottom line - knowing that self-doubt is simply part of the process makes me believe in myself. Now I recognize that when I see another completely put together gal - that self-doubt comes rushing back. But because I know it's coming, I also know that it will go away. My trick is learning how to make it go away faster.

For me, it's talking with a friend who makes me laugh and yes, I'll admit it - as horrible as it sounds - hearing that the perfect are not so perfect after all. That's a hard admission for me because there is nothing I hate more than how we tear apart celebrities, politicians, sports figures and other heroes - that's simply destructive for all of us. But gaining in wisdom as we remind ourselves that we all face challenges is a different conversation - and we all know that difference.

For you, getting rid of your self-doubt could be doing your most favorite thing, giving a hug; it could be taking a run with your dog or volunteering to help someone out.

You see, when we connect with someone else or the world in a way that we love, we remember that we are worth it. Worth it and needed in this world in some way. And once I figured out how easy it is to get rid of self-doubt, I stopped wallowing in it. Instead of days in a funk - it can be an hour or two or just a few seconds. But remember, the key is to know that this too will pass. So, keep from focusing on it and here's the counter advice of the century - no need to discuss and share.

I hear from some that believing ourselves comes with age. The older we are the more at peace we become. That makes sense. It probably has something to do with experience. Eventually, we all figure out that life has ups and downs. We are here for the ride. We are meant to be here. We make a difference. But life is a rollercoaster and we've got to learn to go with it and love it.

Joyce M. Ross – Vancouver, BC
www.grannytakessides.com

Joyce M. Ross is the co-founder of Kindness is Key Training & Publishing Inc.: home of the bestselling HEARTMIND WISDOM Anthology Collection. She and her mission partner, Patricia Connor, are also the co-creators of HEARTMIND EFFECT: Aligning Purpose, Platform & Profit.

Among other published works, Joyce is the author of *Direct Selling: Be Better than Good-Be Great!* (Pelican Publishing, U.S.A., 1991) and *The Kindness Ambassador & the Sugarholic Prosecutor*. Her books can be purchased from Amazon.com and at http://www.heartmindstore.com. She can be contacted via email at info@heartmindeffect.com.

The Power of Hope
Joyce M. Ross

I declared 2015 The Year of Hope. Though *Kindness is Key* is the name of the training and publishing company my good friend Patricia and I co-founded in 2010, as I owe my happiness to *hope*, I thought it was time to celebrate this powerful little four-letter word.

"I hope the dog's going to be all right," Patricia said one bright afternoon while we were solving the world's problems over a cup of tea. A few weeks earlier, Charlie, her nine-year-old English Labrador, was sent home from the animal hospital in the late evening. The vet feared the four-legged-love-on-paws would pass away in the dark and alone.

"You sound doubtful," I responded as Charlie rolled onto his side and stretched out on his bed. Sleeping peacefully, he appeared healthy and content.

"I thought you declared 2015 the year of hope!" Patricia retorted, her hazel eyes lit with mischief.

I laughed. "You know darn well that any sentence that begins with 'I hope' contains an element of doubt."

"Okay, I'm worried. Did I say that better?" Friend for decades, her exaggerated snarky snarl didn't faze me. I thought about retorting with the cliché about how cute she looks when she's angry, but didn't.
"I sometimes worry too," I confessed. "But as long as he's eating and pooing and drinking and peeing, I

choose to believe he remains our *miracle* dog." In reality, Charlie was born a *lemon* dog. As a puppy, he barfed up a variety of processed dog food, leading Patricia to put him on a raw food diet. A few years later, fearing that diet was partially responsible for his near fatal pancreatic attack, he was switched to cooked chicken, vegetables and rice.

Charlie also has Adison's disease. Unable to produce the hormones necessary to calm him, he needs daily doses of steroids and to be kept in a peaceful environment. Now older, he has diabetes which is controlled via insulin injections. Cataracts in both eyes, he's eighty-percent blind. Thanks to the adoring care of Patricia, her husband and an extremely kind veterinarian, Charlie has enjoyed a normal dog life, one miracle at a time.

"What if he gets sick again?" Patricia asked, seeking comfort, not answers. More than once we'd talked about how sad it is that the life expectancy for dogs hovers around a decade.

"Then we'll deal," I answered. "Right now, let's just enjoy him. Worrying about tomorrow is no way to live today." It was the same advice I gave my siblings when Dad was dying. There would be plenty of time for crying when our father left this life for the next. His final weeks were filled with love and laughter, not fear and sadness. His send-off celebration was a mixture of tears and hilarious "that was Dad" stories. After the service, thunder clouds blackened the bright blue sky and spit gobs of rain everywhere. Dad was not happy to be leaving. We cried buckets.

"I guess you're right," Patricia said, not sounding entirely convinced. But as Charlie jumped up, tail wagging, his half-bent ears flopping about like a nun's habit in the wind, we knew it was his meal time. Our world summit break was over. Patricia left the room to feed him. It was time for me to get back to writing.

Writing is a business. Like all businesses, there are facets of it that are enjoyable. Marketing isn't one of them. However, those of us hell bent on not sleeping in a cardboard box, tattered tent or rusted-out van, begrudgingly do what's necessary to sell our work. Unfortunately, rejection is an author's primary ROI. In return for hours invested authoring and promoting, we get rejected, time and time again.

Hardly comforting, but a good truth to know, is that most artists endure similar ego and financial battering. Brush to canvass, hands in clay, fingers procuring sound from an instrument or wrapped around a microphone, creators are a hungry bunch. Starving artist, or not, beside the love of creating, there is a primary force that inspires most of us to continue producing—hope.

A far distant second to fame or riches, we hope that people will gain pleasure from our creations, or that we'll impact humanity in a positive way. Without fully realizing it, no matter their occupation, people spring into action when hopeful, and idle or stall when feeling hopeless. Whenever there is a brass ring within sight, we take charge of our destiny and act.

Should we miss or spend time dangling from that golden circle, we despair. Spinning or stuck, we wait for some external circumstance to change, or for some thing or person to rescue us. When our knight, guardian angel or windfall doesn't materialize, we feel hopeless and give up.

Unlike modern-day man, our ancestors didn't fret themselves into inaction. If food and water weren't readily available, they planted gardens and dug wells. If the land proved barren or dry, they relocated entire villages to more fruitful areas. Giving up was not an option, therefore, inaction was not an option.

Here's the crux of why I dubbed 2015 the year of hope. Hope is the impetus of positive change. Like our ancestors and the animals, regardless of how hopeless your predicament might seem, to overcome challenge, lack or despair, you must act in ways that renew hope.

There is a subtle difference between having hope, and hoping. *Hoping* insinuates doubt. Having *hope* equates with unshakeable belief.

For sixteen years, I ran a Saturday night singles

dance business. The first two years were fun but lean. Full of hope, or an unshakeable belief, that I'd one day build it into a sustainable income, to help pay the mortgage in the meantime, I shared my home with a roommate and rented my backyard parking spaces to a nearby restaurant. All week long, I made hundreds of phone calls to clients reminding them of the next dance and expressing my hope that they'd attend. I sold what was a very successful business in 2010 to pursue my writing career.

For years I dreamed of becoming a freelance writer. Between 1981 and 2007, I wrote five romance novels, and one-by-one, sent each to Harlequin. Every time a rejection slip arrived, I'd get discouraged and shelve my dream for a couple of years. Fearing that I lacked talent wasn't what stalled me. In 1991, Pelican Publishing published my book, *Direct Sales: Be Better Than Good-Be Great!* What did temporarily derail my ambition was that I did not wholeheartedly believe I'd eventually succeed. I forfeited hope.

Ironically, it wasn't until I lost nearly everything—my house, self-respect and sense of worth—via a gambling addiction that I fully appreciated the power of hope. What I didn't lose was my belief that I could recover my finances and emotional health. Being in my mid-fifties wasn't daunting, it was inspiring. Whatever I chose to do to recover financially, it had be something I enjoyed and could do late into life.

It's ironic that when my life seemed most hopeless, by

refusing to abandon hope I ended up fulfilling my lifelong dream of being a fulltime freelance writer.

How cool is that?

Joyce Stewart – Westbury, NY
www.thelovebusiness.net

Joyce C. Stewart is known for her poetry and plays, and is the talk show host of YouTube Channel "Brides and Wives". She is also founder of The Love Business, which provides wise counsel to men and women needing a helping hand in the area of relationships - especially in the love category.

In 2012, she debuted her first book, The BBQ: Fireworks Spark; it was well received. Since that time, the sequel, The BBQ: Lover's Holiday, has stirred up even more excitement. Joyce is more than a romance novelist but also travels to do speaking engagements and women conferences.

Joyce plans to release the next edition of "The BBQ trilogy" in 2015.

Free to Love Me
Joyce Stewart

Learning to love me has been an uphill journey. I believe that there is a process that must happen anytime you consider love. There are no overnight success stories.

I grew up as an "only child", raised by my mother and father until they separated due to a very dysfunctional environment. Therefore, my ideals, identity and self-image were distorted leaving me with painful memories. This was the foundation of the first, most impressionable years of my childhood.

Now that the building blocks of my world were disjointed, my soul began to leak, long and search for the perfect love. The kind of "love" that promises joy, acceptance and "happiness". The type of love that we watch in Disney movies that always end in "Happily Ever After."

Throughout my teenage years, I dated as any normal high school girl and made plenty of mistakes and choices due to such a deep desire to feel love. I gave away my heart and virtue prematurely to one who most likely may not even remember my name.

After I left my mom's house, determined to be independent, I married a man whom I considered to be my best friend, and the father to my children… alas my unconditional "love."

After twelve years of a tumultuous relationship in marriage, we decided to call it quits. I joined the statistics of being a struggling young, black and single mother.

Once my children were old enough to make their own decisions and become responsible, my search for love continued.

This time I was more astute and less vulnerable. I had decided that I would be in charge of my emotions and make sure that I would not end up being a victim as I was before. Still, the more I tried to control the reins of my heart, the more I was disappointed at the end results of any relationship that I entered.

I didn't realize that the problem wasn't the guys that I had chosen even though they were not the best options. It slipped by my seemingly rational thinking that my views and perception of love was faulty. What was I doing wrong????

There became a breaking point in my life that God had to interrupt the "scratch in the record" so to speak. He had to stop me from not loving myself. God preceded to take me on a hiatus of "love discovery" and from that moment forward I began to understand self-love.

As a result of my broken state, I knew I had to renew my relationship with Jesus. I could no longer play on the fence or use God as the unsung Hero in my life. I had to give Him all of me. I had to trust Him to take care of all of the issues and chaos that was driving me to live recklessly with my heart.

One may ask, how does this all tie into coming to love oneself?

Making God the center of my life was only the start of

who I understood myself to be; it is hard to love someone who is a stranger, even if that stranger is YOU.

Yes, I looked in the mirror every day for years and never saw my image from the proper perspective. Knowing characteristics about myself was fine but it did not make me feel special or unique. I needed a reason to believe that I was worthy of being loved and accepting love.

The problem was that I was trying to love myself from the outside in when I needed to love myself from the inside out. I wanted others to love me based on what I could do or provide rather than who I actually was inwardly. I wanted people to love what they saw, and appreciate all that I had accomplished.

Hollywood and Society has trained us to wear designer Guess dresses, Jimmy Choo shoes and Prada bags. Couple that with pink dipped French manicured tips, ruby kissed mac lips, drawn in arched eyebrows and a weave that can be flipped on your sexy hips! Although these are all stunning visuals, and for sure the average guy will stop in his tracks just to take in all of your beauty – BUT when he looks beyond that, will he discover an inner "Beauty" within the outer Beauty???

I confess this was part of my issue. Not that I'm against looking altogether lovely but what I am against is being so busy working on the woman that people can see versus building the "Queen" within who holds your destiny and dreams - life's fulfilling keys.

Through trial and error I learned that loving one's self is about awareness and sacrifice in service to others. If you can understand that you are a treasure created by a Creator who identified you with a fingerprint that no one else has and an assignment that no one else can fulfill, you can own your own space in this world. You can do miraculous things because you are simply YOU.

My journey to loving myself involved my ability to **"know"** myself intimately.

The essence of my truest nature was like the butterfly who was hidden in an unattractive cocoon until its core was perfected. Then when no one was watching - it broke out, stretched its wings and flew into a world that was bigger than any man could imagine.

My life is filled with the pursuit of a wonderful writing career, speaking engagements, as well as counseling and mentoring women. Recently, I started my company called "The Love Business." This is the parent company that umbrellas all of my media centered arts.

This has been a worthwhile experience knowing I'll never have to wait for someone to love me anymore because I AM FREE TO LOVE ME!!!

Karen C. Brown – Houston, TX
www.browncopublishing.com

Karen C. Brown is a native of Louisiana and a 1982 graduate of Grambling State University with a degree in Social Work. Her first book entitled, *If The Tree Could Talk, (oh what stories it would tell)*, was published in 2009. It was followed up by her second title, *Waiting*, in 2013.

Karen loves to read, and is co-founder of Sisters Sippin' Tea Literary Book Club, Houston, TX Chapter. She has always had a love and joy of reading and to date, romance novels are still her all-time favorite. Karen finds that writing is a wonderful way to express oneself as well as a great stress reliever. She is currently working on her next novel, entitled Reconstruction After Ten (an incredible breast cancer journey). The release date is tentative for Fall 2015.

Learning to Love Me...After Breast Cancer
Karen C. Brown

It was the spring of 2000; I had a fairly hectic schedule. I was juggling the duties of wife, mother, daughter, sister, friend, and employee. I worked at a nursing facility where I worked as a social worker. I must admit, it kept me very busy. Dealing with residents as well as staff could at times be very challenging, but for the most part I enjoyed what I was doing and like to think that I made a difference in some small way. I had the privilege of coming home in the evening to my second job. Even though I didn't earn a penny, it was the job which was the most fulfilling.

One day, I discovered a lump in my right breast. It was on the far right side and I could feel it at times when I would put my arm down at my side. I wasn't overly concerned about it since I have a history of a fibrocystic breast (tissue in the breast that feels lumpy) and this wasn't the first time I had felt a lump. Actually, this made the third time I had a lump, and each time I had a biopsy it always turned out to be nothing.

After a few weeks, still not bothered but at the same time thinking I needed to get it checked out because I wouldn't want to feel this lump in my breast indefinitely. The only way for it to be removed was to have it done so surgically. I eventually made and appointment with my Primary Care Physician (PCP), who encouraged me to get a mammogram by saying, "since we don't know what it is, it would be best to get it checked out". I scheduled a mammogram with the next few days, still thinking I was wasting my time. Besides, it always ended up being nothing.

The morning of my mammogram at the imaging center was uneventful. I didn't have to wait long to be called in the back for the exam. I have had mammograms in the past; I don't like them. I bet any amount of money this machine was developed by a man who evidently thought it humorous in some way for a woman to have her breast mashed as flat as a pancake.

Historically, the person doing the exam never talks or says anything much while doing the exam other than the occasional "can you stand here, put your arm there, take a deep breath.....let it out." I even try to read their faces to see if something in their expression warrants a cause for concern. They don't give anything away, nothing. Stone faced.

Not the case on this day. The woman who did my exam was talking to me about what she was seeing. As she finished the exam she said, "I see something, not sure if it is cancer or not, but whatever it is, it's early. When you go get this checked out, make sure you see a Breast Surgeon. You don't want to go to just any old body, go to a breast surgeon." I just sat there and listened, still not thinking much about what she was saying.

A few days later, I got a call from my PCP's office

telling me to make an appointment to see her so that we could go over my results for the biopsy. In my mind, I was so sure all would be well that it never registered in my brain for things to be any other way.

I went to my appointment and boy, was I surprised when my PCP told me I would need to schedule a biopsy and then she would have additional information for me. I don't know what I was thinking. Maybe she was going to write me a prescription that I could pick up at the pharmacy that would cause the lump to go away on its own.

One day at work, as I was walking through one of the units heading to my office my co-worker stopped me and if I would look at her insurance statement she had received regarding her prosthesis. I had no idea she was wearing one, or that she had breast cancer. She looked normal and natural to me. I reviewed the paper work with her and we talked about it for a bit and she went on her way.

I still needed to make an appointment for my biopsy. I had yet to find a breast surgeon; I was kind of dragging my feet. I was in no hurry and if the truth were known, by not progressing to find the doctor I needed it allowed me to be in that place called denial. Eventually my co-worker and I talked about what was going on with me and she shared the name of the breast surgeon she had seen and how great he was. She gave me the information and encouraged me to call him soon. I promised I would.

I eventually made the appointment to meet with the breast surgeon. By the time I was scheduled to meet with him he had received the copy of the x-rays from the imaging center. The x-rays were discussed and the surgeon expressed he was not concerned about the lump because he felt it was a big cyst. His concern was for what could not be felt, but was seen in my x-ray.

Once the biopsy was done he said he would have a better idea of what we were dealing with. I realized how serious this matter was becoming and felt I needed to make plans to get this biopsy done right away. Before leaving the office, I scheduled my biopsy for the next available time slot. I was beginning to get anxious and really nervous.

Fast forward to after the biopsy. I was told it would be a few days, four or five before I would hear anything back from the doctor. I think everyone knows the drill. If the nurse calls and talks to you about the outcome, all is well and right in the world. On the other hand, if the doctor calls directly and wants to talk with you about the findings, and tells you to bring someone with you when you come to the appointment, we know it most likely time to push the panic button.

I waited and waited for a call that never came or so it seemed. I had exceeded the four to five day mark and was beginning to get a tad bit upset. I felt I was getting the run around and my mind took me to places I would rather not go. I really lost it when I was informed, after one of my calls to the doctor's office that he would be out until after Easter Break. My co-worker encouraged me to call the office again and ask to speak with the doctor who would be following my doctor's patients. To my surprise, I got a call later in the afternoon from my doctor. I was relieved and frightened at the same time. Here was the moment of truth I had been waiting for.

He said, "I regret to inform you the result from your biopsy shows that you have breast cancer". If you have ever watched an episode of the Charlie Brown cartoon, you know the sound that the teacher makes when talking to the kids, that is what I heard that day. I don't know how I was able to talk, let alone respond appropriately, but I guessed I must have. I somehow remember confirming I would be at his office the following Tuesday and would bring someone with me. Again my co-worker was there. I fell apart and caused her to do the same. I calmed down and got myself together to drive home. Once there, I remember being weak in the knees and crying tears from deep within my soul that were filled with sorrow, pain, fear, confusion, doubt, disbelief and a bunch of other things I still can't describe.

By the time I made it home, I was able to get myself together enough to call my husband, who left work immediately. My oldest sister was called next. She too told me she was on her way to my house. I called my baby sister; I wish I hadn't. She has never been able to handle any bad news. She was screaming and trying to talk at the same time. I hesitated on calling my mother, who was ill at the time, but I called anyway. I called my father-in-law who was in Detroit, MI. He wanted to know if I wanted him to come. He didn't hesitate in saying he would.

By the time that Tuesday rolled around for my appointment with the doctor, I was ready. When we got to the appointment and the doctor came in to visit with us, he answered every question we had without even asking them. I knew then and there he was the doctor for me.

I will soon have my 15th year anniversary as a breast cancer survivor. I have a great support system and I have a wonderful Oncologist, and will be his patient for life. I admit that I still strongly dislike going to his office, but it is something I must do. I don't have to like it and I am fine feeling about it as I do. It is just another one of those things in life that just is what it is.

I thank God for the gifts he has given me by way of people; my husband, children, grandchildren, friends and family. On this journey, I have learned to show random acts of kindness, for you never know who you may be helping in ways you may not even be able to comprehend. I have learned to do things because my heart says so and it makes me feel good to think that I could make a difference in someone's life. I have learned to trust God and give him the honor and praise. I thank God for blessing me and keeping me and allowing my moments to roll on a little bit longer.

Kelli Bolton – Columbus, OH
www.kelliwrites.com

Kelli Bolton is a compassionate young woman with a desire to see the Word of God set the lives of his people free. She is a faithful member of Agape Family Worship Center, under the leadership of Pastor Yolanda Tolliver, and is actively involved in ministry. She and her husband Vernon have three children, and are deeply committed to training them up, as Proverbs 22:6 advises.

In 2000, Kelli received a prophetic word concerning writing, and heeded to the call. She was inspired to write a book about teen dating and domestic violence. In March 2009, Kelli published "You Said You Loved Me", demonstrating to young people what real love looks like. In 2012, she released her second novel "Church Gossip", and is currently in production with the film version of the book.

Know Your Worth
Kelli Bolton

There was a time in my life as a young Christian, not knowing my worth that I befriended a young man who I thought was "nice." We met through my doing work in the community. He was nice looking gentleman and, for his age, he was also intelligent. The more I began to work with the young people in his building, the more he and I began to talk.

Now, he told me he was saved and that he went to church, but had not been in a while. Although that did not bother me, and we seemed to have other things in common, it should have been the first red flag I noticed, but I enjoyed his company. Over time, we began to hang out and spend time together. I never felt anything other than close friendship for him, so imagine how I felt when he tried to make a move on me one night. I was shocked and sat there for a minute thinking to myself, "Do I act like nothing is happening, or do I get up and punch this joker in the face"?

I got up and went home, not saying anything about what happened. I never expected this from him because he never showed he was interested in me other than friendship. Sometime later, we talked about the incident and he turned the situation as if were my fault - like I allowed him to do it! I asked him why he thought it was okay to do that, and he said, "I don't know, I just felt the urge." I thought to myself, "What if I just felt the urge to punch you in the throat"?

Once we got past that situation, we had a

conversation about "my body language" and what it was suggesting to him. This particular evening we had gone for a drive and came back to his house to watch television. I felt tired, so I laid across his bed (why did I do that?).

Next thing I know, the lights went out and the music came on. I got up, got my things and headed for the door because that situation made me feel very uncomfortable. As I told him bye, he leaned in for a kiss, and I replied, "Friends don't kiss". Even though he said he knew that, he tried again. I told him "I don't kiss my friends", and left.

The very next day he and I met to discuss some details for a program I was putting together, and he brought up what happened the night before. He told me he had never been rejected before and he did not take it lightly. I told him that I did not think God was allowing me to see him in that way, not that I thought he was unattractive, but God was not allowing me to see him the way that he noticed me. He told me I was lying to myself.

He said, "I can respect what you are saying, but when the opportunity presents itself, I'll be waiting." At that point, he shared his perspective of how I carried myself; how I smiled when I talked to him; how he got the most attention when I came into his building; how other people thought that I was interested in him. I told him that I could care less what other thought, my feelings were strictly platonic.

The funniest thing he said to me was, "you should know how your behind moves when you wear certain clothes". And I thought, "How would I know that if I do not have eyes in the back of my head"? He began to tell me how coming over to a man's house and falling asleep were signs that you were comfortable with him, and that "play fighting" was an indicator that you were interested in him.

I totally disagreed because I used to play fight with guys all the time when I was younger without it being an issue. I was speechless by his remarks; it was as if he was blaming me for his lack of self-control. When I went home, I sat back, reflected on that conversation, and did a self-evaluation of my behavior. Had I been leading him on?

If so, why didn't the men in my office respond that way when we would "play fight"? I decided from that point on to put some distance between me and that guy. I guess he felt like he had met some women who claimed to be Christian, but gave into what he wanted. His goal was to break my will, but it never happened.

The last straw that ended this relationship was when he called me last minute on a Saturday to take him to the airport the next day. I told him I would be in church during the time he needed to be there. He was not happy. When we did talk again he said, "You could have left - you didn't say that your Pastor needed you for anything". Little did he know my church had an obligation with another church later that afternoon. I told him that I did not feel like he respected the relationship he had with me, or the relationship I had with God. He told me that it wasn't about my relationship with God; it was about my being there for him when he needed me.

I realized this relationship had to end; he was not someone who added fruit to my spirit. God had shown me all I needed to know about him. I learned an invaluable lesson as well, to make sure my talk and my walk add up, but most importantly, never let anyone tell you who you are and what you will do.

LaDonna Marie – Savannah, GA
www.ladonnamariebooks.com

LaDonna Marie is an International Award Winning and Literary Author, Writer, Poet, Motivational Speaker and Founder of Planting Positive Seeds #PPS. Her first book, Until Tomorrow Comes, ranked #2 and #3 on Amazon Best Seller in Poetry and Positive Growth, and was awarded Honorable Mention in the 2014 Paris Book Festival in Poetry Category.

LaDonna wants to help address issues for growing children to create an awareness of childhood depressions, low self-esteem, and relationships. Her mission is to empower and encourage others to keep moving forward with faith.

Fighting to be Me
LaDonna Marie

Once I heard the words from the movie, The Color Purple, "All my life I had to fight", it totally resonated with me; because truly, I feel as though I've always had to fight to be understood. The irony is that as far back as I can remember all I ever wanted was to live a life of peace, love and sharing compassion for others. As I look back, one of my most vivid memories was when I was called a hypocrite as a child. Even then I remember the words that came from my mouth, "Jesus said suffer not the little children and let them come unto me".

So there was always something about God that made me feel at peace. Although being that young and not having my positive mindset reinforced or strengthened, doubt began to fester about me, my true purpose, and the meaning of life.

Questions started to arise and I wanted to know if my thinking pattern was right for my age, or if I was wrong for automatically having a genuine love for people and the Lord.

At the time, I couldn't define *authenticity*, but I knew having people question my good heart, and kind actions bothered me, because that is who I knew I was inside. Although I was young, I was outspoken and assertive, which was perceived as being disrespectful and a smart mouth. I just knew that I wanted to be heard, and loved for being me and who God made me.

As the years began to pass, I really started to feel

misunderstood, and as a result I began to withdraw and become defensive. All I kept asking myself was, "Why don't others understand me"? I encountered some negativity and harsh words that made me feel sad and really alone.

Then one day I had a visitation from the Lord; I guess he could see I had all these words on the inside of me that I couldn't get out. I didn't want to ever be disrespectful; I just wanted to be heard. So he guided me into writing poetry to help heal my frustrations, anger, sadness, and broken heart. He ensured me that as I healed, he would one day help me to heal others. So I gladly accepted the charge, not saying it was easy by any means, but I started to write poetry. Poetry became my therapy, my safe haven, and what made me happy. I was only 12, but I wrote every day. I remember one of my first poems, A Gift is Born:

Sitting inside these four white walls
not the padded ones with straitjackets
But this one is secluded and isolated all the same
Thoughts get lost in the air
Confusion stirs from truths unknown
Anguish and anger finds me
See there is no other person present but myself
I begin to bounce questions
to and from counteracting my
Ideas against perceptions
There are frequent interactions
Constantly measuring my reactions
to the distractions that come my way
So I take a seat in the room with
the white walls with my pen and pad
Thus my love for writing poetry begins
A gift is born!

So over the years, I was constantly trying to figure out what was going on in my life. I lived life with a smile plastered on my face as I was still trying to understand.

I was in turmoil thinking no one would ever love me; no one would ever understand me; so what difference did my life make? So I made the decision to try and take it. I based my decisions on the negative words of others, not fully knowing how the others could be controlled by principalities, and evil spirits. So I decided the when, where and even what time to carry it out. I just remember the unbearable pain and being rushed to the hospital.

During my college years I was involved in a very bad car accident, where I lost a friend instantly. I had only known her for a short while, however, she was the most kind, and loving person I had ever met. She helped me to learn to put all my hurt and pain aside and that genuine people do exist. Moving forward in my life, God helped me to understand, that I would surely have my share of good days and bad; but no matter what, He would always be there for me.

Then God began to reach out to me more. He helped me realize that I had to trust him and not worry about the others who didn't get me or understand me. He let me know that I was exactly the way he wanted me to be; created in his own image; fearfully and wonderful made. He basically told me stop trying to prove myself and just be who He made me to be. My relationship with God ultimately helped me start on the path to learning to love me. I truly started to understand the depth of how much He believed in me and validated me over the years. No matter what I had Him in my corner, pushing and cheering me on. I was everyone else's cheerleader and he was mine.

So here it is all my life I was fighting to be the authentic me that I knew I was; but once I found it, I became enamored with finding true love. I set out looking for the person that would help me to fill that void. I was looking for love in all the wrong places, giving my heart away to people that were not really ready for a serious relationship.

Then one day I cried out to God and asked him to help and guide me. So I began to turn inward and learn to love me. I would look in the mirror to encourage myself, saying I could do all things through Christ. I allowed God to heal my broken heart, from all the years I had poured out love and it wasn't given back. He helped me to understand that a relationship with him would allow him to find my true love.

There are moments when I reflect on wanting to take my life, and the many accidents and incidents that almost took me away from this world. But instead of dwelling on it, now, I awake each day thanking the Lord for another day, and I consciously decide to move forward in life. I have days when my conversation with the Lord is telling him I believe. I have devoted my life to help empower others through my writing. I'm glad I've learned to love myself because, who I am now is exactly who I knew I would be when I was younger. God helped me to blossom into who he intended me to be with no holding back. I have learned to love everything about me, and I know I am enough; I am resilient; and my inner strength is powerful based on my foundation in the Lord.

Michelle Poitier – Jacksonville, FL
www.michellepoitier.com

Michelle Poitier is a 13 year U.S Navy military veteran, mother, grandmother, entrepreneur, author, motivational speaker and advocate for survivors of domestic & sexual abuse, homelessness among female veterans, and those battling with Post-Traumatic Stress Disorder (PTSD).

Michelle is the founder and CEO of Future Impressions LLC (http://www.futureimpressions.org), a mobile business providing professional writing services and administrative support. She received her Associate of Science Degree in Business emphasis in computer science at Florida Technical College in October 2006. She completed her Bachelors of Science in Business Management with the University of Phoenix in March 2010.

To Bring Hope Where There is None
Michelle Poitier

Last year, at the age of 43, I hit rock bottom. I lost my apartment, car, and relationship with my parents. With no home of my own, I was forced to live with friends. My life was in a rapidly downward spiral and suicide appeared to be the only way out.

Every day, I was looking for a reason not to commit suicide. I had a suicide plan in place. I had planned it. Four bottles of prescription narcotics resting by the bedside was going to be my escape from this life.

After spending thirteen years in the US Navy, I left military service in 2003 due to a heart condition and a medical disorder eventually diagnosed as Post Traumatic Stress Disorder or PTSD. According to the US Department of Veterans Affairs, PTSD can occur after an individual has experienced a traumatic event such as combat, sexual or physical abuse, serious accidents, or natural disasters. The agency's statistics show that between 11 to 20 percent of veterans of the wars in Iraq and Afghanistan experience PTSD. Women are more likely to develop PTSD than men because they are more likely to experience sexual assault and child sexual abuse. I am one of those women.

I am a survivor of military sexual trauma, and also sexual abuse prior to my military service. After leaving the Navy, it was increasingly difficult for me to just get out of the bed each day. The things that I enjoyed, I wasn't enjoying anymore.

My first sexual assault occurred when I was six years

old. An uncle tried to rape me while I was sleeping. I thought that it was a dream. When he was finished, the last thing he said was if you tell anyone, I will kill you. I felt terrified and alone; my mother was away in the military, and I was being raised by my grandmother. A couple of months later, a second uncle exposed himself to me.

It took several years to tell my grandmother about the abuse, and when I did, she rebuked the story...so I never mentioned it again. At the age of 16, I was raped by one of my mother's military colleagues at a party, and said nothing. A year later, I tried to commit suicide by taking pills, but a friend intervened and rushed me to the emergency room. It saved my life.

The military was meant to be an escape from the past, but, it wasn't. While serving in the Navy, I was raped by a colleague who was supposed to be a friend. Again, I kept quiet; I didn't even tell my fiancé whom I later married.

I was tired of lies and secrets because secrets hurt. So to overcome what happened, I tried to excel at everything during my naval career. However, by the time I left the US Armed Forces, I was a broken woman.

The sexual trauma has impacted every aspect of my life. It has impacted my relationships, finances, and every step of my life. My marriage eventually ended in divorce.

On the verge of suicide, I confided in a friend about my turmoil. The friend also was a veteran and told me about No Barriers USA (www.nobarriersusa.org), whose mission is to release the potential of the human spirit. The organization devotes most of its resources to helping veterans break through barriers and find their inner purpose through journey based expeditions that range in length from one day to three-weeks. These "Soldiers to Summits" expeditions have taken veterans to Nepal, Ecuador, Peru, the South Pole, and locations across the United States. I credit that organization with saving my life. No Barriers gave me my sense of purpose back, and made me believe that I could achieve my goals; they saw my potential.

In 2013, I joined the "Soldiers to Summits" program and traveled with a team to Peru for a two week expedition. The trip involved hiking eight hours to reach the remote community of Q'eros, located on the eastern side of the snowcapped Vilcanota range of the Peruvian Andes Mountains. Portions of the community reside over 16,000 feet above sea level.

The team spent several days painting a school in a village that had almost zero contact with the outside world. Although I was trekking through some of the most challenging mountain terrain in the world, I was terrified of heights. There were a couple of times I thought, "Michelle, what have you gotten yourself into"?

Next, we hiked for two more days until we reached summit of Mariposa One, over 16,000 feet above sea level. That experience was life changing. It was absolutely amazing. Nature has a healing quality that medications don't have for me. So "Soldiers to

Summits" was literally my lifeline because I was done. I had literally given up.

One year later, I am an entirely different person. I now live in Jacksonville, Florida, and am pursuing my goal of public speaking and confronting the stigma of sexual trauma. I really found out that I am a fighter. My self-esteem and identity were restored because I had lost it all. Now, my next goal is to complete a project that will house homeless female veterans with children. The way that people reached out to me when I was at my lowest point encourages me to give back, inspire, and give hope to people that felt as hopeless as I did. Just to be able to bring a gleam back to someone's eye, hope where there was none, is what drives me.

Norlita Brown – Atlanta, GA
www.facebook.com/norlita.brown

Norlita Brown, a Detroit native, holds a BA in English from Georgia State University. She is the co-founder of Brown Essence, Inc., a boutique publishing company whose works depict the truth in reality.

Brown is the co-author of two works of poetry and one collection of words of wisdom. She is the author of three novels and a collection of short stories. Brown's work has also been included in an anthology brought together by Kendra Norman-Holmes as well as the award-winning anthology by National bestselling author, ReShonda Tate Billingsley, *The Motherhood Diaries*.

Lady in the Mirror
Norlita Brown

I had been sitting at the vanity in my bathroom mirror for nearly an hour; most of the time was consumed with thoughts of who I was. At this moment, I hated me, or maybe I should more correctly say, who I had come to be. My journey wasn't easy, it was a long hard, painful road, but I climbed the mountains, pushed past the boulders and now here I stood as the Vice President of a conglomerate where many people could only wish to be a minion. Yet, I wasn't happy.

Happiness had long since left me behind, even though I smiled everyday like we were the best of friends. I mean honestly, why wouldn't I be happy with everything laid at my feet, accessible to me by the touch of my fingertips? Men wanting to wine and dine me, women hating the very thought of me. Jealousy oozing through their bloodstream the moment I stepped into the room with my head held high, clothes made from the finest designers, diamonds cut from the best rock and yet none of it was real.

The value placed on them with dollars and cents diminished tremendously when I thought of the last time my smile was genuine, my heart was full, my eyes danced. The last time my laughter filled the air with thoughts of goodness. I had changed who I was to become who they wanted and they loved it, but I didn't.

I laughed at those who mimicked me; trying to become the person I was, trying to achieve my level of success. Clawing at paths I once traced, following me on social media to see what moves I would make.

If only they knew the depths of their decisions. "BE YOU!" I wanted to scream at them, the things I've done, the person I've become is not for YOU, hey, it wasn't even for me.

So, now here I was sitting, staring at the image of me that made the cover of many magazines, the layouts of their feature articles and all I wanted to do was cry. I glanced at the make-up that made me over, the foundation, mascara and lipsticks, the glosses and tweezers that plucked my eyebrows into that perfected arch and that's when it happened, the tear that left my eye, ran down my face, smearing my flawlessly placed foundation, lightening the space that was once beautiful and revealing the space that wasn't. It continued its trek until it landed on the counter mixed with a variation of colors. That tear was for me. It was a reminder that this wasn't me. It showed me that no amount of make-up could really change the person that God created, that the "make-over" was really in His hands.

The next tear that followed was angry, because now I would have to start this forty-five minute ordeal all over again. So, I let them flow, each tear owning a different meaning, a different revelation.

"Do you need some help in there?" I heard him call out for at least the third time since I had begun.

Anger took over my senses as I shouted every pain of that moment.

"If I need your help, I'll let you know!" I snapped.

"Excuse me?" he said as if I needed to rethink my words and try them again. He was wrong, because in reprocessing came another lash out.

"You heard me correctly the first time."

"What did I do to deserve you speaking to me in this manner?" he asked indignantly as if I owed him something. He was now standing in the door way, his reflection now joined mine in the mirror. I didn't turn to face him; my eyes caught his in the mirror.

"The same thing you always do, nothing!" I snarled, my lips curled involuntarily but they matched my feelings perfectly. I was disgusted with him, though I really didn't know why. Every pain and every hurt, every person that ever caused it was now balled up into this one man, so he would be my punching bag, because they were no longer here. They weren't standing in front of me asking to "help" me - words that my mind interpreted as, "use me, change me, make me" it most always represented something bad.

"I do nothing for you," he said as his temper now rose and entered the bathroom, coming toward me with hurt in his eyes. Still, I wouldn't face him. "Everything I do is for you, how dare you try to diminish what we have, who I am, what I've done."

"What have you done?" I asked nonchalantly as I shrugged my shoulders indifferently.

"I have given over 15 years of my life for you, that's what I've done," he said as he poked his index finger in the air emphasizing every word while never disconnecting his eyes with mine. "I've made sure you had everything you needed, everything you wanted to become who you are today. I've made sacrifices, borrowed money, lost friends along the way, for you. And now you want to sit on a high horse like I didn't help put you there and look down on me."

"How can I look down on someone who sits so high?" I asked, sarcasm dripping from my every word as I waved my hand in his direction.

"Where is this coming from?" His tone had changed, the anger was gone, in its place was a voice of reason, the sound of sadness, but my moment hadn't passed. He didn't know that I was in a moment of transition, a moment that was revealing to me a person I despised. It wasn't him, it was me, though if I said those words it would be cliché.

"It's coming from you," I screamed as I now stood and turned to face him. "It's coming from every time you made me feel like the real me wasn't good enough, my hair texture, the length of it or the lack thereof. It's coming from every time you made me feel my eyes weren't bright enough, my smile wasn't wide enough. It's coming from you," I paused as I turned and faced the mirror once again. The truth in my words hit me hard!

There was a boulder on my chest now and I couldn't breathe. Everything I said was true, but I was directing my anger at the wrong person, that is until I turned back to the mirror. No one can make me feel like I'm not good enough but me, their thoughts and opinions of me didn't matter or at least it shouldn't have outweighed my own. I was the one who failed me, failed to see my own beauty, my own worth. I did this to myself.

I fell back into my seat, my shoulders heaved over and I cried. He walked closer to me, knelt down beside me, picked up the make-up cloths and began to gently wipe away the foundation, and eye liner, the lip stick and eye shadow. When he was done, he gently slid the wig from my head, taking the net off with it. He unbraided the locks I had just put in and then he stood behind me and placed his hands on my shoulders.

"This is the woman I fell in love with 15 years ago, the same woman who I love so much today. Now, it's up to you to love her, too. I can't do for you what you need to do for yourself, I can only show you how," he said as tears ran down his own face.

"Then why would you let me do all of this?" I wasn't letting up. I was still placing blame, though in my heart I really just wanted to make sure that he really loved me.

"I didn't *let* you do anything. I loved you with every flaw, every imperfection, with or without makeup or your hair styled. *I love you!*"

I faced my image and breathed. I let out a heavy sigh that contained years of self-hatred, I wiped the tears from my face and I repeated the words my husband said. I LOVE YOU! I said to my image softly, then louder. I reapplied my eye makeup, but decided against the foundation, glossed my lips, fluffed my hair out, stared my reflection in the eye and said, "I love you, just the way you are. The beauty you own flows deeper than what the eye can see."

"Agreed," he said as he hugged me from behind then

turned me around and kissed me.

"Thank you for loving me," I said.

"Thank you for finally loving the woman I love, I can't wait to see what she's about to do."

Renee Bolton – Chicago, IL
www.beautyschoolscarlet.com

Renee Bolton is a beauty maven who exudes splendor in all things beauty! Author, and creator of Beauty School Scarlet, her purpose is to empower women and girls to make the best choices in life to improve their lifestyle from head to toe as well as from the inside out.

The brand Beauty School Scarlet is more than a beauty blog; it is a movement to inspire women and girls to be beautiful while promoting and affirming them throughout the course of their lives. She encourages them to realize that, "beauty is not complicated or complex; it is simple."

Never Give Up
Renee Bolton

It's been over ten years since my divorce but I will never forget the day my then husband left me almost homeless. But before I spill the tea, let me give you the short version of what led to this almost unfortunate situation.

From the outside we had the "picture perfect" marriage, a five-bedroom home, two-car garage, a Mercedes and no kids. We hosted parties with family and friends on a regular basis; I was a "Real House Wife" before there was a show! We worked hard but we played harder. There was always a party on Hunter Green Lane.

Things seemed to be going good but something was truly missing. We both wanted more with our careers but only one of us could step into a new direction. Being the loving husband that he was, he agreed that I would step out on my own as an entrepreneur.

I decided to use the money from my personal savings and 401K to get the business going so I wouldn't disturb the household account. As soon as I withdrew the money and quit my good job with benefits to start a home-based business, things started to change! That's when he changed.

For two weeks things were great. We celebrated my new move as an entrepreneur, he helped with the setup of my office and then he came home one evening and said, "We need to talk". Out of nowhere, he stated that, "he filed for divorce." Yes, that's right, he filed - not consulted with a lawyer, but filed for a divorce. He said, "He was never in love with me!" I was surprised, upset and devastated. I actually thought he was playing but he was dead serious. I could not figure out why or what went wrong. What did I do to make my husband fall out of love with me? I had to find a way to make things better. I was determined to make it work.

We said our vows and made a promise to God, so I had to save my marriage. I cut off all my friends and put all I had into this man. I decided to go into overdrive with my marriage. I cooked every day, I cleaned 24/7 and I gave up the goodies EVERY NIGHT! Yes honey, he was not going to leave me without a fight. But, he did! He left me with a five-bedroom home, two-car garage, a Mercedes car note and little money in our joint account.

He packed up all his stuff in the middle of the day while I was out and moved back with his momma. He left me high and dry with all the bills. No note, no phone call; nothing! I cried, I prayed, I prayed and I cried then I soon realized that he was not coming back and he refused to help me. He would not take my calls, he acted as if I never existed and he sent me a message stating that he didn't owe me anything. No explanation, nothing.

I could not believe the man I fell in love with would disrespect our love, our life and my heart. But, with prayer, faith and family, I pulled it together. After realizing that I could not change a man, I stopped feeling sorry for myself and I moved forward with my life. I gave up my business; I got a job, moved, gave up the car and restarted my life. Although my heart was broken, I learned to bounce back and live for me.

I learned to love myself and not make a man my everything. I learned to enjoy my own company and enjoy my beauty from the inside out!

I'm sure you may be saying, "How can you be happy after an unexpected divorce? How were you able to bounce back?" And my answer is, it's possible over time with self-evaluation, self-love and self-empowerment.

Now don't get it twisted, all these self-things were not easy. The struggle was real but most importantly I did not give up! I was forced to look in the mirror and ask myself a few questions, "What was my contribution on why the marriage ended? Could I have been a better wife? And how will I get through this and get my happy back?"

I knew this would not be an easy task but it all started with me being honest and true to myself. While I was not the perfect wife, I was a good one. Yes, there were things I could have done better and more; but I could not change the past. Once I gained an acceptance and understanding of that, I was ready to move on.

The key was learning from my past so I could prepare for a brighter future. I didn't date immediately as I did not want a rebound guy or end up with divorce #2. It actually took me two years to get back on the dating scene. I took some time to get to know me.

I needed to understand what made me happy because at the time I was depressed. I spent a lot of time alone in my feelings and thoughts with and without prayer. But when I started dating, I had fun!

Once I started to get to know myself again, life became easier and I had an epiphany. I realized that I lost myself in my marriage. I did everything for him…meaning my life and dreams revolved around him and his happiness. Instead of standing up for myself, doing some of the things I wanted to do; I became the woman he wanted me to be. It was then that I asked myself, "When was the last time you were truly happy in life?"

The day that I answered that question is the day my life changed! That was the day I found my happy after my divorce and I have been living it up ever since!

My advice for anyone who is currently in this situation is to know and understand, that this too shall pass because you are amazing! Be brave because you will learn, laugh, love and live again…I did!

Please note that going through a divorce is not the end of your world, it is the beginning of a whole new world for you. Take time to do all the self-things; self-evaluation, self-love and self-empowerment. After you re-evaluate your life and take time for you, you will be ready to move forward to the next phase, which is forgiveness.

Always remember to let go and forgive yourself of past hurts and mistakes. Holding on will weigh you down and keep you from moving forward. It's called the past for a reason!

Holding on to past hurts and mistakes will have you running around in the dark trying to find your way to the future stumbling along the way. What purpose does it serve to hold on and be angry? It only hurts you and holds you back from moving forward. Let go; move on and find your way to a promising future! Look at past hurts and mistakes as lessons learned to grow and flourish from. Allow yourself to heal so you can live, learn, laugh and love again!

Let your happiness be your sanity; allow your happiness to keep you going. Life is too short to hold on to things you cannot change. Move forward, do what you feel and don't live life without regrets.

Serena Wadhwa – Chicago, IL
www.triqualiving.com

Serena Wadhwa, Psy.D., LCPC, CADC, is an assistant professor/program coordinator at Governors State University. She provides individual and group therapy at the Alexian Brothers Outpatient Group Practice.

Dr. Wadhwa works in a variety of roles as a consultant, creator, presenter, trainer, lecturer, radio talk show host and author. She is currently on a different path and is working on figuring that out. Yoga, writing, comedy, awakenings, and the extraordinary are definite parts. And ashrams. Well maybe just a couple more of those.

Giving Me a Chance
Serena Wadhwa

Love is one of those words that mean so many different things at so many different times to so many different people in so many different ways. And there are so many levels of love. For me, I've learned that the process of loving myself was just that, a process. It was something that happened in small steps, over a period of time, as I slowly became ready to experience this truly wonderful place, without fear, without judgment, without conditions. Many steps had to happen in order for me to be ready to awaken to this level of loving myself that I currently embrace.

What was the initial experience where I learned it was necessary to love myself? I talk about this particular experience when I present on mission statements and values, as I was trying, as the time it happened, to make sense out of a senseless experience. For the first time in my life, I found myself completely alone and I had to learn to love myself at some level, because there was no one there but me. Let me backtrack a bit to give the bigger picture.

Decades ago, I was in an abusive relationship with a man from a different race. Being from a traditional East Indian family, being in a relationship with someone from another race was not acceptable. When I discovered I was pregnant, this was a second taboo I committed. I violated many cultural norms for the times and subsequently paid a high price for these perceived cultural insults. I long ago realized that what was right for me did not "fit" into the cultural proscriptions my parents wanted me to abide by (which was the source of much of our disagreements and of course for many individuals caught between two worlds, a story for a different day) and thus, braced myself for whatever "punishment" they were going to bestow.

At the time I decided to keep the baby, this was mainly because the baby's father convinced me that he was going to change his ways and be the person I wanted. Of course, being young and naïve at the time, I believed him, because, that's part of the process and part of the experience of being a young adult. I don't know what "would" have happened if I had loved myself differently and made a decision on what was right for me rather than what was right for us (aka-him). At that age, I thought I knew better, and in reality I didn't. When I was eight months pregnant, the baby's father left me.

At the time, I was living in a motel and working two jobs to support us (he did not work) and when he broke up with me, I realized that I was going to be raising a child on my own. That was a pretty scary realization. I had to go to work that evening (I worked at a restaurant as a server) and I remember one of the other servers coming up to me and asking me what was wrong. She was able to tell that something was wrong and I told her what happened. Now keep in mind that at the time this happened, this woman did not like me. She thought I was a spoiled Indian brat.

After telling her what happened, she felt sorry for me and told me I could move into her home. Of course, initially, this was awkward. Yet after a few weeks, as we slowly got to know each other, we began developing a really close friendship. In fact, she was going to be in the delivery room with me.

Tatiana was born on September 22nd. Adjusting to having a tiny person fully dependent on you and losing your independence on a different level was a completely new experience. I also knew that in order to take care of her, going back to school was going to be in the picture, as having a degree would provide some sort of employment.

I decided to go to a university that was close to where her father was staying, as I didn't want to deny her knowing who her father was. Whether her father was going to be a part of her life was a decision she was to make, the only decision I was to make was whether she was safe around him.

I made the transition to a four year university, which in itself was another huge adjustment. Finding a daycare, deciding how to take classes, working or not working, how much financial loans to take, these were all things I needed to consider and these were overwhelming, as I had little to base my decisions on and little to compare them to. Yet, finally, in January the following year, off to school we went.

Three days into the semester, I found myself at the town hospital, where the doctors and nurses were trying to inform me that Tatiana was dead. She had passed away from Sudden Infant Death Syndrome (SIDS), or crib death. At the time, there wasn't much known about this particular syndrome. I was in shock, as I was in disbelief this was happening. How could it be happening? Especially after everything I had gone through to get here? It didn't seem fair. My family was called, my best friends, and I had left a message for Tatiana's father. Yet none of it made sense to me. How could it? How does it? Is it even possible?

After the services, Tatiana's father and I met several times to talk about her. I shared some of the milestones she made (she was about 3 ½ months when she passed). We bonded, of course, and I remember after several meetings, there was talk about getting back together. I had to think about this. After all, he left me when I most needed him and while at the time I perceived that as a betrayal, after I had Tatiana, realized it was probably for the best.

Tatiana did not need to be around the chaos that was part of his life. I had also gone back to school, which had always been a part of my "big picture" and was realistically impossible with the relationship I had with him. When Tatiana was born, she helped me get out of a toxic relationship and back into school. Was that something I was going to risk and if so, was the reason valid?

After some consideration, I decided that getting back together was not the best thing for me. I wanted to honor the path I was brought to because of my daughter and didn't want her death to be in vain and if I chose to get back together with him, I had no certainty that I was going to stay in school and keep my sanity. So I set a boundary and said good-bye.

While that process was painful and lasted for a period of time, it really was the catalyst of learning to love myself. It set in motion the series of steps I needed to face in order to truly learn to love myself and not allow myself to be compromised. In my journey, I have learned that love transcends and is unconditional. It doesn't mean I will allow someone to repeatedly hurt or abuse me; however, it does mean giving people a chance, and that includes myself.

Shelia E. Bell – Memphis, TN
www.sheliaebell.net

Shelia E. Bell (formerly Lipsey) is an award-winning, national bestselling author with over a dozen books published in Christian fiction, women's fiction, and young adult genres. Her books have garnered many awards, including 2015 Rosa Parks Award, 2014 Christian Literary Award, AAMBC Nate Holmes Honorary Award, Kindle Award, OOSA Book of the Year, and numerous others. In 2012, she founded and hosted the Black Writers and Book Clubs (BWABC) Literacy Association and Festival.

Shelia is the proud mother of two sons, one who stands by her side in the publishing arena and serves as the Chief Operating Officer of their newly formed independent publishing company, Bonita and Hodge Publishing Group. She also proudly proclaims the blessing in the form of three grandsons and two great granddaughters.

I Remember the Time
Shelia E. Bell

I guess some people would say that I have had a pretty weird, sometimes sad, sometimes crazy life. If you know me, if you really, really know me, you would say that my life has been one long, never ending roller coaster ride. I would definitely agree with them (whoever *them* happens to be).

Like Gladys Knight sings, "I've had my share of life's ups and downs." But you know what? I can finally say that I have had my exhale moment. There have been many ups and downs for sure, and I have risen to the occasion each and every time. I cannot give credit to myself because that would be boastful and prideful. I can only thank the one True God who I know has brought me through over and over again.

Let me tell you a little about myself so you can perhaps understand me a little more and the reason why I feel so divinely blessed today. Those who are familiar with me, or who have perhaps heard me speak, know that at the age of eighteen months I underwent open-heart surgery. Six months later at the age of twenty-four months, I contracted Polio.

Polio is a highly contagious viral infection. It can lead to paralysis, breathing problems, and many died from it at the time I contracted it. Although it is mostly eradicated now, except in some third world countries, it has left its lasting effects on me and my body. The type of polio I have is sometimes called spinal polio because of its ravaged attack on the motor neurons in my spinal cord, which caused paralysis in primarily my right leg and my left foot. I walk with a limp, wear a brace and use crutches to help me ambulate. The polio also caused my lower extremities to atrophy, leaving my legs exceptionally skinny.

I grew up in a loving, stable home, but the thing about it is I was hardly ever present in my home. I spent most of my young life in and out of hospitals, sometimes having to be there for months on end. I even went to school in the hospital. I missed out on many events and special occasions with my family. Many memories my three older siblings have, I have no recollection of.

My parents instilled in me the importance of living an independent life. My father was disabled due to World War II, where both of his legs had to be amputated below the knee after shrapnel lodged in them. So there were two of us in my household with disabilities.

As a child and teenager, I was often ridiculed, teased and tormented because I was different. Sometimes kids, especially boys, would follow me around pointing, and jeering at me, laughing at me and talking about my skinny legs. Needless to say, I went from being a little girl who thought she could do anything anyone else could do to being a teenager who felt ostracized, different and self-conscious. I was the only person in my entire school (elementary, middle and high school) that had a physical disability - so imagine how I stood out! Don't get me wrong, I had friends and I was quite popular, but inside I felt less than, self-conscious and not good enough. I was always going about trying to prove to my peers that I was just as good as or better than them.

As a woman, it doesn't seem to take much to think of myself as not good enough. Sometimes I allow outside interferences to creep inside my mind and I become this weakened vessel who thinks I don't add up or can't pass the tests that life often whirls my way. As a result, I've entered into unhealthy relationships or acted in manners that were less than pleasing. But I realized that I was made to succeed in this world…no matter what others said or how they treated me.

As I grew older, my feelings of inadequacy mounted. On the outside, I wore smiles, I excelled in school, I always managed to get great jobs and have a successful career. But on the inside, I was tormenting ME.

I had my first born at the age of sixteen. The father of my child, after *his father* told him there was no way he could have a crippled girl pregnant, just quietly disappeared out of my and my son's life. I think he would have tried to re-enter into our lives had he not gone off on the wrong path in his life, but that is a totally different story.

Two years later, I was married and got pregnant with my second son. His father was violent and physically abusive toward me. I became one of those women who remained in the marriage until I realized that I had to get out of it for the sake of my sons. I wish I could tell you that was the last time that I was physically and emotionally abused, but unfortunately, it was only the beginning. You see, no matter how much I succeeded in my career as an administrative assistant, no matter how many friends I had, no matter how blessed I was to have two wonderful sons, I still hated the person I was.

I just couldn't quite understand why God allowed me to have polio. I couldn't understand why I had to wear the braces, use the crutches, have skinny legs and limp. Because of my parents, I grew up believing in God. I grew up being taught that God is love! I grew hearing the song, "Yes, Jesus loves me," but the older I became, the more I thought that God couldn't possibly love me or he wouldn't have let me contract polio. On top of that, I wondered why, if He loved me, did he allow only mean, abusive men enter into my life to hurt me and destroy my spirit? I didn't understand it.

It took me years to come to the realization that God really did and does love me. All that I have gone through in life, all that God allows me to go through even now, is what makes me who I am. Every single thing, whether I caused it, accepted it, whether the devil meant it for harm, God used to propel me!

I went on to marry two more times and divorce two more times! Each marriage was far worse than the one before. The abuse escalated until I feared for my life. Yet, I still thought that these were the only type of men for me.

Sometimes without realizing it, I subconsciously brought forth those things that I dwelled on in my mind. Words are powerful, and form from thoughts; whether good or bad, when those thoughts are released into the atmosphere, they can bring into existence those very things we detest (or love).

I had to learn through difficulties and abuse that I was the one drawing these lowlifes into my life with the way I felt about me. I had not learned to love myself, so I thought that I was unworthy of being loved and treated with respect, kindness and affection. I had allowed my physical imperfections to rule my mind and in return, I drew all that negative junk into my life like a magnet.

It was only by God's amazing grace that I came to realize later in my life that I am uniquely made. I am one of a kind. I am amazing. I am smart. I am talented. I am gifted. When God made me, He knew exactly what He was doing. He made me perfect. He made me able to withstand to persevere and to love.

After all the years of feeling sub-human, God has allowed all the things I went through to mold me into the person I am today. My latter days are proving to be better than my former days. However, I believe I had to experience and go through much of the things I went through in order to become the woman of God that I am today.

Tavetta Patterson – Gary, IN
www.publishinglife.wix.com/pattersonsglobal

Tavetta Patterson is a public speaker, award-winning mentor, and philanthropist. She is the author of *The Tongue of Life, The Secrets We Keep,* and *The Bridge that Brought Me Over.*

Tavetta is the President of Abundant Life Publications, which provides communications consulting; leadership development; as well as book and magazine publishing. She is also the Director of Gary Life Education Initiative Incorporated, a nonprofit organization that empowers students for life through mentoring; providing leadership skills; and career readiness.

Married to husband Roosevelt, the Patterson's desire to help people discover and live their purpose.

Finding the Me to Love
Tavetta Patterson

The journey to learning to love me began during a conversation with a teenager. I told her, "When you love yourself you will not allow anyone to abuse you." Her response hit me like a ton of bricks. She replied, "I don't know how to love myself." I wondered how did we get to a time and place where teenage girls didn't know how to love? Then I was reminded of my teenage years.

At the age of sixteen, I encountered my first personal experience with domestic abuse. I was in a relationship with a guy who learned abuse as a method to control girls. I was certain that my life would never travel this path because I saw my mother endure domestic abuse when I was a child. I remember repeating to myself on a very consistent basis, "No man will ever hit me." Each time I saw my mother get beat it caused an indescribable pain. It caused me to have very confused thoughts about the true meaning of love.

I remember hearing the men who beat her say, "I love you and I'm sorry" so they could be allowed to move back into our house. However, it was always a repeat of one fight after another. Each encounter showed me what I did not want for my life. With each slap I watched my mother endure, it caused resentment within me because I did not have a father present to protect me.

I moved out of the house with my mother when I was sixteen years old. I was not sure of where I was going or even what I wanted in life. Nevertheless, I knew I could not endure the environment I was living in at that time. I walked out of a house where there was a constant abusive relationship and walked directly into an abusive relationship. It is a sad but true reality that often times what we are most familiar with is drawn to us.

The abusive relationships that I walked into lasted from the time I was sixteen years old until I was twenty one years old. The moment I really discovered and understood who God created me to be, I walked away from love abuse and love abusers. Love abuse occurs when a person uses the language of love, but the actions of abuse. Love abusers usually specialize in charming words, but deceitful actions.

The journey to love me was filled with bumps, bruises, twists and turns. However, I am so glad that I lived to share my life with others. Some of the experiences I endured caused other people to lose their mind, end their life or injure the person who caused the pain. I am so glad that I encountered God as my keeper. I have a promise which I still confess on a regular basis, it is Philippians 4:7, "And the peace of God, which surpasses all understanding, will guard your hearts and your minds in Christ Jesus."

In addition to reading the word of God I began to read books like, "Lord, Teach me How to Love" and "The Bait of Satan." Those books were tools that helped me receive deliverance from offence and bitterness from all those years of abuse. I learned that it is the will of God to love and to be loved. I learned that my past could not dictate my future as long as I was willing to surrender to the plan of God for my life.

Writing is another outlet that I use to learn how to love me. It is an outlet that allows me to share the love of God with people around the world. My first book was written from a place of pain and a desire to be healed.

I submitted a poem to my high school English Teacher during my senior year. She submitted the poem to a writing contest. It was selected as a winning poem and published in a poetry anthology. In 2002, it became the first poem in my first book entitled, "The Tongue of Life." The following year I recorded a spoken word cd of love poems.

Then I began volunteering at a local shelter to help women find their voice and tell their story during a creative writing class. Many of the women had survived domestic violence and it was a full circle experience. Volunteering at the shelter helped me to understand that everything intended to harm me, became a testimony that I shared to help other women. I learned that love is what kept me in the midst of all the trials and tribulations. I learned that we have the power to change our life and experience love on a high level.

At twenty one years old I made the decision to practice abstinence and cut off every connection I had made with men who did not truly love me. I began praying and attending a regular bible study with a group of strong women. Those decisions led to more mental and spiritual clarity. As a result I gained understanding of my true identity. I discovered through the word of God that I am loved. I discovered that I am the apple of God's eye. I discovered that God loves me so much that he gave his one and only son for me. I discovered that I could love me and that would be enough. I learned that God is the best father I could ever have in life. I learned that there was a husband tailor-made for me. I learned that I had to clear my life of the old counterfeits so that real love could walk into my life.

At twenty three years old I married a man who loved me unconditionally. The love that God allowed me to witness through my husband has taught me how love thinks, acts and speaks. The love I experience on a daily basis between God, my husband and I, is a miracle. The love I have discovered in this stage of my life has given me the wings to soar in my personal and professional life. God has allowed us to mentor children; to share the gospel and travel around the world spreading His love.

I was able to grow in a restored relationship with my mother. I learned to love her at the capacity she was able to handle love. In return, she gave me love at the capacity she was able to give love. My mother passed August 5, 2013. I am thankful to say that she passed peacefully. There was not anyone near her to hurt her anymore and God fully restored the love in our relationship.

During 2014 I was able to begin therapy. It provided an opportunity for me to talk about the abuse I endured as a teen and the abuse I witnessed as a child. I learned what it really means to love me.

I learned that you can never conquer what you are not willing to confront. I have confronted my past; conquered all my fears; healed from the pain of love abuse and made a commitment to love me and only allow people in my life who love me unconditionally.

August 2, 2014 I was able to share my journey to true love through the release of an inspirational memoir entitled, "The Bridge that Brought Me Over." The bridge that carried me over every negative encounter in life is God. Today, I love myself so much because I had to fight a spiritual battle to learn how to love me. Now I will not allow anyone into my life who displays signs of abuse. Now when I speak to people about love, I can confidently say, "I love me" and really mean that statement.

The best way to learn to love yourself is to seek your original manufacturer, God. What I have learned is that when we look to the world to define who we are, there will always be confusion. When we seek God, we discover the original plan for life. The love of God is patient and kind. People who enter your life should operate with the same type of patient and kind love. In reality, to know God is to know true love.

Toneal M. Jackson – Chicago, IL
www.weareaps.com

Toneal M. Jackson is a married, mother of many, who also happens to be an International Award-Winning Author; publisher; ghostwriter; speaker; mentor; licensed evangelist; and youth leader. As an author, Toneal writes books in the self-help, inspirational, and children's genres. In 2012, CBS Chicago recognized her as one of "5 Indie Chicago Authors and Publishers to Watch Out For".

She is the founder of Authors Promoting Success, an organization that provides an array of services to educate independent authors about the literary industry and assist them in accomplishing their goals. In May 2015, Toneal opened her bookstore, APS Books & More, which she deems as being "Home to the Independent Author". Located inside of Chicago's Ford City Mall, this unique book boutique offers Spanish classes; tutoring; workshops; story time; book signing opportunities for authors; and more.

The Most Valuable Lesson Learned
Toneal M. Jackson

Although writing this anthology was my idea, it was very difficult to gather thoughts to compile into a story. Not because it's not a topic in which I can identify; but because I can identify all too well. The fact is that for me, there was not necessarily one particular incident that gave me to know that loving myself was essential; it was a process that took years, and many trials and hardships before it totally seeped in.

All my life, I have truly struggled with embracing self-love. I've always demanded a lot from myself, because that was the standard that was instilled from my childhood. The expectation in my household was that you get good grades, and do your chores well; being pretty or loving yourself was not really taught – instead, I think my parents thought it was implied. It's funny how the things that we purposely try to teach are not necessarily the lessons that are learned!

So needless to say, I was always an honor roll student (I had no choice if I wanted to stay out of trouble); great at sports; and could keep a house like none other – I've been cooking since I was nine. And as I grew older, the standards that were initially provided by my parents, inherently became my own.

Once I got to high school, no one had to tell me to study, or do my homework; I knew that if I wanted to watch television, talk on the phone, or go out with my friends that it, and my chores had better be done. However, in retrospect, I wish there were times where I was told to look in the mirror and tell myself that I was beautiful, and that I mattered; the truth is that it took me well into my adult years before I understood this to be true. I mean, I was considered one of the popular kids in school, and I always attributed it to my intelligence, and ability to be the "go to" friend – you know, the one you can tell your secrets to, or truly be yourself around without being judged.

And maybe being trustworthy, dependable, and smart were great characteristics to possess; however, I never thought anything of it because I felt alone. Don't get me wrong, I had friends, and to this day, I thank God for my best friend because there were many times that her advice got me through my situations, but I just always felt as though I didn't matter. That the only reason I had friends was because I was smart – not because I was pretty; not because I was important to them, but because if ever they had a problem, they knew that I was not only capable of finding a solution, but I was good at it.

Some people may look at that as being used, but to me, it gave me a sense of purpose…and that was something that I desperately needed.

I was the one who felt like having a boyfriend was required, well maybe that's not the right word, but if you had one, you must have been pretty – you must have been important because otherwise, how could you have a significant other, right? And the fact that it was a long while before I actually had one (worth having anyway), I believed was a reflection of my character; as though it was something wrong with me. So for a long time, I guess you could say that I was depressed, although I didn't classify myself that way…just empty.

I remained being everyone's "go to" person, and by the time I finished high school, my execution was flawless. I could iron my dad's uniforms; clean the house; go grocery shopping with or for my mom; get my homework done; help everyone else with theirs; go to practice and perform well; and still get home in time to watch my favorite show on television.

By the time I turned 18, I was a sophomore in college. I thought that everything would change because now I was officially grown. I was working and going to school, both on a full-time basis. I really had no time for a relationship, but it was something I longed for because I still felt that there was something missing.

I ended up dating someone that I really liked, and was surprised that he liked me – in that way. I mean, I was always the friend, never the "chosen" one. So we dated for a bit, and before long got engaged. I felt that it should be the right thing, because now I had someone showing me the love that I thought I always wanted, right? However, something was still missing. I mean I liked him; he was a great guy – any girl would have loved to be with him. But something in me couldn't truly give my heart to him, and I ended up breaking off the engagement.

So I'm still living my life, or shall I say, going through life every day the same way. Get up; eat breakfast; brush my teeth; shower; go to school; go to work; study or do my homework; and go to bed. Sounds pretty boring and mundane, doesn't it? But that's what I'd grown accustomed to – that's all that I thought I deserved. Living a good life was for the pretty people, the ones that everyone else liked and admired; which, from my perspective automatically implied that I would never live a good life. I finished college, with honors, but what else was to be expected? I mean, being smart is who I was raised to be.

A couple of months before I graduated, I'd gotten engaged again (to a different guy). Not long after graduation, I found out that my mother had cancer and was not expected to live long. So needless to say, I got married a few months after receiving that news. Who needed to spend years planning a wedding? My mother was dying, and I wanted her to see me walk down that aisle.

So I got married, and a couple of months later found out I was pregnant. This would be my second time being a mother, as I was initially bestowed this gift upon marrying my husband; he already had a daughter, and I received the privilege of parenting her.

Much of my life was spent taking care of others – my mother (until she passed away); my children (I gave birth to four girls, plus the oldest one we already had); my husband; his family; you name the person and it seemed I attended to them…everyone that is, except myself.

I suffered through a series of strokes; over the course of 10 years, I'd had three major strokes, and probably a dozen minor ones. I grew tired of spending so much time in the hospital, with every diagnosis disproved. I began to pray and ask God to reveal what was going on with me, and more importantly, what I could do to prevent it from recurring.

I slowed down on my activities, telling others "no" as I awaited His response. It seemed as though He wasn't answering; the irony is that the more I slowed down, the better I began to feel. The more I told others "no", the more I saw that the world didn't end, and they still loved me. So I'm still waiting to hear from God when I realized that He'd already given me my answer.

I had to learn to take time for myself. I had to learn that I couldn't be everything to and for everybody – and that was okay. People didn't just love me for my contributions to their lives; those that did, God gave me strength to leave them alone.

I learned that even when I couldn't walk or talk that I was still valuable, because I needed me. I needed me to get better. I had my own goals that I still had to achieve. I had girls to whom I needed to impart wisdom.

I appreciate my life now because I play an active role in it. No longer am I solely concerned about everyone else – *their* feelings, *their* needs, *their* desires. I matter, because now I matter to me.

What's ironic is that I still make a lot of the same choices, but now it comes from a different, happier, healthier place. The decisions I make, I no longer resent. No longer do I require validation from others to know my worth – inside or out. I now know that I am beautiful and valuable, regardless of what others may think, because I have learned to love me.

Conclusion

Loving yourself isn't about how smart you are, or contrary to my belief, how beautiful you are. Loving yourself isn't about how many tasks you can accomplish, the amount of work you complete for someone else, or even the accolades you acquire.

Loving yourself is about embracing who you are inside. The good; the bad; the shortcomings; the achievements – accept the fact that all of that is what makes you unique. Your beauty is not based upon esthetics, rather your character. What you achieve in life should be based on what makes *you* happy – not what pleases someone else. At the end of the day, you have to face yourself in the mirror and be okay with what stares back at you.

Unfortunately, loving yourself can't be "taught", but is definitely a lesson that needs to be learned. Its importance should be encouraged and embraced. Loving yourself provides empowerment. Loving yourself provides confidence. Loving yourself provides courage. When you can love yourself despite your mistakes, flaws, and failures – then you are truly destined for greatness.

It is when you love yourself that you can properly and positively love others, and walk in your purpose!

Other Books by These Authors

Amani Jackson
Mommy's Sick Day
I'm A Big Boy Now

Carolyn Gray
All About ME (Manners & Etiquette)
365 Days of Gratitude: There is always something to be grateful for

Chelsea Duggan
The High-Five Hound

Dominique Wilkins
Giving My Tears A Break
Theresa in Wonderland

E. J. Brock
Brock's Redemption
A Spirit Mate Series

Freda Emmons
Resurrection Hope
Flame of Healing

Haleh Rabizadeh Resnick
Little Patient Big Doctor

Joyce Ross
Granny Takes Sides advice column

Joyce Stewart
The BBQ Series
Somewhere Amongst the Rainbow

Karen C. Brown
Waiting
If the Tree Could Talk

Kelli Bolton
You Said You Loved Me
Church Gossip ~ also a movie

LaDonna Marie
Until Tomorrow Comes
Shattered Pieces of Me

Michelle Poitier
Releasing the Pain
Random Thoughts from the Heart

Norlita Brown
Destroying the Mask
The Last Shall Be First

Renee Bolton
#ImBeautyInspired

Serena Wadhwa
Stress in the Modern World

Shelia Bell
My Son's Wife Series
Fairley High Series

Tavetta Patterson
The Bridge that Brought Me Over
From Mourning to the Morning

Toneal M. Jackson
Pleasing Your Partner: A Spiritual Guide to H.A.P.P.I.N.E.S.S.
Inspiration from A.B.O.V.E.

www.ingramcontent.com/pod-product-compliance
Lightning Source LLC
Chambersburg PA
CBHW061438040426
42450CB00007B/1119